THE BACK
OF BE

By Sheila Hawkins

A **KYRIAKOU** BOOK

Copyright © 1995 Sheila Hawkins

First published in 1995 – paperback edition
by K.P. Kyriakou (books & stationery) Ltd
P.O. Box 159 Limassol, Cyprus
Telex 2836, Fax 05-371706 ✆ 05-368508.

Illustrations © Harry Hawkins

Distributed by **KYRIAKOU BOOKSHOPS**

ISBN 9963-571-51-4

CONTENTS

PROLOGUE

1971 and a posting to Cyprus! Those were the glorious sun-drenched days and moonlit nights with a whole island to explore. Clear, sparkling sea where our children dived and swam like fish and turned golden in the sun. Mountains and *mezzes*, kebabs and *kokkinelli*, barbecues and squadron parties. Learning the language and enjoying the overwhelming hospitality of the local people.

Tears in 1974 as we left after the coup, leaving behind a divided and tragic island, a lot of friends and an intrinsic part of ourselves.

1980 and we are posted back to Cyprus! This time we do not visit the occupied north. Instead we revisit the isolated Akamas area, wild and beautiful and mainly uninhabited. We fall in love with the place and its people and acquire a piece of land in a secluded valley surrounded by carob and pine trees and overlooking Chrysochous Bay and the mountains beyond.

We now have a dream. One day we are going to live in paradise at the back of beyond.

CREDITS

My thanks to the many friends who helped and encouraged me in this first attempt at writing; to Ian Mair and Graham Parsons who introduced me to the world of computers and to my husband, Harry, for his unflagging support and superb illustrations.

DEDICATION
For our children.
May they never lose their sense of humour.

CHAPTER 1

THE BACK OF BEYOND

I stood on the deck of the channel ferry and watched the English coastline disappearing into the mist. Gulls wheeled overhead, their mournful cries fading in the wind, as the boat ploughed steadily through the slate-grey water. A fine drizzle soaked my hair, droplets trickling down my face like cold tears, and a feeling of melancholy enveloped me as I thought of my family and the familiar things I was leaving behind. This time, there was no going back - the move overseas would be permanent. I stared into the churning wake, my thoughts in turmoil. The resonant blast of the ship's siren jolted me out of my reverie and the fleeting nostalgia left me. One last look back and I was ready to move on. France lay ahead - there was a continent to cross and foreign lands to explore.

It was the summer of 1984. Harry, having requested an early retirement, had finally left the Royal Air Force and at the end of May, we had driven down to RAF Manston in Kent, for a final farewell in the Officers' Mess, before boarding the ferry at the start of a journey that took us leisurely across rural France, avoiding the main towns and staying in well-run country pensions and auberges. Here we learned to play Piquet and were challenged to many a game of boule by the local clientele. In one unforgettable place, when they learned that Harry was an officer with the Royal Air Force, the bar filled up and an impromptu party began - red wine flowing as fast as the wartime reminiscences of the RAF and the maquis. On up into the French Alps, where snow still clung to the mountains and the air was crisp and clear, to linger awhile on the shores of Lake Annecy and indulge ourselves with magnificent strawberry tartlets and steaming bowls of café-au-lait in the early morning chill at Albertville. Then swiftly through rain-soaked northern Italy and down the Adriatic coast, eager to reach Ancona, where the MEDITERRANEAN SKY waited to take us on the sea voyage to Patras in Greece.

Once aboard, with the car safely stowed below decks, we toured the ship and, having dined well, retired to our comfortable cabin for a surprisingly good night's sleep. We woke to clear skies and a calm sea and, before long, I found myself once again standing on the deck - this time not looking back, but ahead to the new way of life that lay in wait for us. Long gone were the grey waters of the English channel. Here, iridescent bubbles formed and flowed past as the ship's bow sliced through mermaid-green depths. The creamy bow-wave rose and curled back and, suddenly, a school of dolphins was escorting us, their beautiful, sleek shapes leaping and diving through the streaming water. They stayed with us until we approached the mainland of Greece then, as swiftly as they had appeared, they were gone - leaving us entranced and gazing towards a shoreline where the water turned to peacock-blue, shot with emerald and turquoise, and sparkled like a million diamonds in the early morning sun.

We disembarked at Patras and, with time to explore this historic land, headed into the Peloponnese; to Ancient Corinth and Olympia, where, in 776, the athletes of the first Games had challenged each other and the Olympic flame still burned brightly. We gazed from the castle walls at Castro over green fields, splashed with the scarlet of poppies and the bright, golden yellow of marguerites glowing in the warm air and clear light. Then back to Athens to marvel at the Acropolis and hold our breath as the sun set through the marble pillars at Sounion, before boarding yet another ferry, at

Churches of Byzantium.
Byzantine Church.

Piraeus, which would take us back to our beloved Cyprus.

Like a leaf randomly cast into the water, Cyprus lies at the eastern end of the Mediterranean. It is a land of sunshine and fair breezes, of history and legend. Fertile valleys and pine-clad mountains, of spectacular beauty, lead on all sides to the brilliantly blue sea. Castles and churches of Byzantium, mosaics and ancient monasteries beckon the traveller and everywhere there is evidence of past civilizations. It is an archaeological dream come true. In spring the ground is carpeted with wild flowers and the song of the nightingale fills the air. In summer, westerly breezes cool the coast and clear, warm water laps the shore. Mountain roads lead through pine-covered slopes to Troodos and the Paphos forest where, in a densely-wooded valley of majestic blue cedars, wild moufflon roam and eagles soar. In winter, snow falls and the mountains are transformed as thickly whirling flakes muffle the ground and shroud the trees in an eerie silence. When the snowstorms pass, the untouched expanse of glistening whiteness against the blue sky is beautiful beyond imagination. Ski runs are opened and log fires blaze in mountain cabins. Below, on the salt lakes, massed clouds of pink show where the flamingos have returned to their winter feeding grounds, their reflections in the silvery-green waters one of the lovely sights of Cyprus. Fruit has ripened in the citrus groves lining the coastal roads and golden oranges glow brightly among the dark, glossy leaves of the heavily-laden trees. The enduring people of this troubled island are hospitable in the extreme and, in the more remote villages, their warmth and friendliness to the stranger is unsurpassed. It was to one such village that we had come to make our home.

We had arranged to rent a small house in the village, where we would live while we built our own house a

There was a young one tethered outside.
Donkey in window.

kilometre or so down the road towards the little fishing port of Latchi. Arriving after dark, we found the house easily enough from the instructions we had been given. It was a modernized village house with quite a large garden, planted in front with lemon and almond trees. The key having been left in the door, we entered to find there was no electricity connected. However, we had a torch and the first priority was to find the bathroom. We were in a hall which had a table, four chairs and a big stone fireplace. Doors to the right and left led to a bedroom and a kitchen. Our hearts sank - there was no bathroom. Harry opened the back door - panic over - there was a bathroom, complete with flushing lavatory, they just hadn't told us you had to go out into the garden to get to it. This was to prove a mite inconvenient in the winter when it was lashing down with rain, not to mention having to run the gauntlet of next door's cockerel, every time you needed a bath. Nothing could dampen our spirits though, we wound ourselves in some clean sheets and fell, exhausted, on to our new bed. We were here to stay.

Just before dawn a cockerel crowed loudly outside and the challenge was immediately taken up by all the others in the village. Then the real dawn chorus began in earnest as the donkeys (and this village was famous for breeding them) started up with an ear-splitting cacophony rising to an almighty crescendo. "My God" said Harry, his head under the pillow, "you'd think they were in the room with us". A fresh blast assaulted our eardrums. They WERE in the room with us - there was a young one tethered outside with its head poking in through the open window. With a final snort the impudent head withdrew, to be replaced a moment later by its owner's head, clad in a battered cloth hat.

"Kalimera, kalosorisete", he bellowed, in a voice a mere decibel or so lower than his donkey's. I grabbed my sheet as the head disappeared and the clanking of buck-

This was Theodoulos.
Theodoulos.

ets accompanied an endless tirade of incomprehensible Greek as he fed and watered his donkey - one of several as we were to discover later. This was Theodoulos, brother of the owner of our new home who was currently resident in Australia. He had a proprietary air about him and we guessed that a small thing like a couple of tenants in the house was not going to make any difference to his use of the garden for his livestock.

Fully awake now and eager to explore our new domain, I elected to shower first and, looking nervously around to ensure I didn't have an audience, I dived across the open space between the back door and the bathroom. There was plenty of water, it was even tolerably warm from the solar heater, but I had to share the shower with a bright green tree frog, which hopped disconcertingly around by my feet, and I emerged clutching a white pigeon, which came in through a small window and perched on the towel rail.

Harry fared slightly worse. By the time he got in there, the neighbour's marauding cockerel had worked out there was an intruder on its territory and had positioned itself by the door, strutting menacingly up and down and hurling itself at him, in a raucous fury of ruffled feathers, every time he tried to put a foot outside. It was weeks before we realized that the outward-opening door could work to our advantage, but, thereafter, a violent push from inside the bathroom would fling the malevolent rooster half way across the garden, while we made a wild dash for the kitchen door.

During that first day a steady stream of hospitable people came to welcome us, bringing gifts of olives, olive oil, tomatoes, cucumbers and loaves of freshly-baked bread. From next door the neighbours brought *haloumi,* a local cheese made from ewe's milk, and a bottle of still warm goat's milk. The parents were shepherds who lived, with their huge flock of sheep and goats, in a big cave near a deserted Turkish village while their eldest daughter stayed at home to look after her brothers and sisters.

We walked up to the coffee shop to renew our acquaintance with the *Mukhtar*, or Headman of the village, whom we had previously met during negotiations for our land. We were surrounded by the villagers we had come to live amongst - those having been introduced earlier, now experts on our age and number of children and passing it on to the newcomers. The coffee shop began to fill up and we were shaking hands with people called Peracles and Socrates, Calliope, Aphrodite and Antigone. "*Kalosorisete*" "welcome", they said over and over again. The pungent smell of burning olive leaves came from a *kapnistiri* carried by the taxi driver's wife, Vassilou; and we were instructed to draw the smoke in towards us with a circular motion of the hand. "Holy Smoke!" said Harry, wafting it towards him, while everyone made the triple sign of the Cross in the Greek Orthodox manner. This would cleanse us of any harmful spirits lurking about and ward off the evil eye.

As dusk fell we sat outside the front door by the lemon tree, sipping brandy sours and listening to the sound that was to become so much a part of our lives, the monotonous cry of the little Scops owl. The Cypriots call these small birds "Johnny" and their soft hoot does sound remarkably like someone calling for a lost John. Of course, being Greek, the local people have woven a legend around them and the neighbour's daughter told us the story.

There were once two brothers, John and Demos. John looked after his father's sheep and Demos looked after his father's horses. One night, as they prepared to shut the animals in, they counted twenty four sheep, but only twenty three horses. An argument ensued, during which Demos struck John and, accidentally, killed him. He then realized that he had forgotten to count the horse he was riding and was stricken with remorse. He was about to end his life when the Gods on Olympus took pity on the boy and changed him into a bird, forever destined to wander the earth at night, searching and calling for his dead brother, John.

As one who loves Greek mythology, I find these legends and superstitions and beliefs a delight. Everything has its explanation, its reason for being the way it is. Here the people were still close to the earth - donkeys were the main form of transport and ploughing was done by oxen and a wooden ploughshare. The day of the Japanese 4-wheel drive was not yet upon us.

CHAPTER 2

NO PROBLEM, MRS SHEILA!

The ensuing weeks and months found us integrating more and more into village life, while every day we went down to our land. One day two men from the District Land Office came to mark the boundaries. The total area was a little over two thirds of an acre on, mainly sloping, ground running down into an old *argaki* bordered by a dense thicket. Lambis, the man who had sold us the land, had, in previous years, tried to terrace and level it to grow winter feed for his donkey, but the ground was steep and very rocky in places and he had no access to water nearby. As he grew old the land remained unworked and dense scrub had taken it over again. On the high side the boundary was marked by a line of beautiful, dark green cypress trees, some tall and slender, others with widely spreading branches. All down the lower side, bordering the stream-bed and the track, were carob trees and, behind, dominating the border furthest away from the sea, was a very old, truly magnificent pine tree. Standing more than a hundred feet tall, its lovely branches stretched endlessly out into the blue sky. Although this tree is in the next field, it has self-seeded into our garden and the tallest of these new pines on our border now stands about twenty feet high. In front, the valley sloped gently down towards the sea, the dark green foliage of carobs and cypresses contrasting with the light, bright green of pines and the pale silvery leaves that crowned the gnarled and twisted trunks of ancient olive trees. With the surrounding slopes clothed in evergreen bushes and scattered carob trees, we had an abundance of pleasant greenery around us, providing a secluded area in which to build a simple house that would not spoil the environment. We drew plans of the site and spent hours mentally landscaping and planting trees and shrubs, so that, when the ground had been prepared and the final position of the house determined, we could begin planting in earnest. First, however, there was a lot of hacking and clearing to do and then, with his huge bulldozer to level the site, came Kleopas.

Kleopas was a powerfully built man of few words and a completely bald head. In those days he had the only big earth-moving machine in the area and he drove it with unreserved determination. No land was too inaccessible, no hill too steep. He was fascinating to watch, if you could bear it, as he stood the thing on end, seemingly defying gravity and roaring around the site like a monstrous wall-of-death rider. Gradually some lovely natural rock was uncovered on the border with the cypress trees. Kleopas was all for dynamiting this and getting rid of it, and shook his head in wonderment at the strange ways of foreigners when we timidly said we liked it.

After much discussion and planning, Harry had finished designing a simple, but functional house. We intended to build on two floors, with the living area upstairs and the sleeping quarters down; firstly to take most advantage of the magnificent view and, secondly, to keep the bedrooms cool in summer. We envisaged a large living room, overlooking the bay, with sliding picture-windows opening to verandahs at each end, a big natural stone fireplace and an archway into a simple kitchen. This is exactly what we built and now, almost ten years on, as I sit on the front verandah writing this, I am as enchanted with the view as when I first saw it.

Work began and it was not long before we began to discover a few snags in the lateral thinking of some of the local building experts. The day dawned when the house

Its lovely branches stretched endlessly out into the blue sky.
Pine Tree

was to be laid out and the foundations dug. Yiangos, our builder, arrived early. He was a short, stocky man with iron-grey hair and an engaging grin. He had a family of beautiful daughters and his main purpose in life was the provision of dowry houses for them as was the Cypriot custom. He, and the architect who had drawn up the plans, pored over the drawings and in came the digger to excavate the foundations. This done, they poured in some concrete and left it to set. We wandered down in the evening, to admire the beginnings of our future home, and Harry stood looking thoughtfully for a while before slipping quietly back to the village for a set of plans. He had discovered that the house had been laid out back to front, so that the front door would open straight into the solid rock formation behind. Realizing that this might interfere with our social life, the following day we duly pointed out the error to our maestro. Unperturbed, he gazed at the tricky situation.

"No problem" he said.

With hindsight, we should have been suspicious long before this, as these words were about the sum total of his spoken English. After a few weeks, the only time we ever really began to worry was when he said "no problem" and, by then, we were both working in T-shirts with these immortal words emblazoned across the front. Despite having one or two other things which weren't a problem either, like leaving out an entire ground beam (which forms an essential part of the basic framework of the house) and constructing a septic tank which wouldn't hold water, the house progressed - these minor hiccups taken in his stride by Harry as he, and various friends, beavered away at terracing and building retaining walls.

I was appointed general factotum and kept pretty busy. Being the better at Greek, one of my main tasks was interpreting and pouring oil on troubled builders when

Lurching and wheezing up the dirt track came a contraption.
Ruston Bucyrus Driller.

their ideas didn't coincide with ours. Slowly we built up a relationship of friendliness and respect with the local workmen which has lasted to this day, and extends to their families who include us in all their major celebrations.

One day Yiangos informed us that the machine would be coming to dig the soak-away pit for the septic tank. We had previously seen these formidable red lorries in Limassol. Mounted with massive cranes and screws, which drilled deep bore holes into the earth, they were manned by teams of highly efficient men in matching red overalls and, rather impressed, we awaited its arrival with interest.

An enormous rattling and clanking and series of explosions heralded the arrival of our driller. Lurching and wheezing up the dirt track came a contraption, the sight of which left us both speechless. It eventually came to rest in what would be our front garden, coughed, spluttered, exploded and, finally, died. It had obviously been a thing of past glory, for a plaque attached to the side bore the famous name RUSTON BUCYRUS of Lincoln. It had none of the niceties like doors and windows, no number plates and only the tattered remnant of a seat for the driver. The starting system was long defunct so they started it by topping up the carburettor (which had no cap) and connecting a couple of wires to a battery, which sat where the passenger seat had once been. At the back a rickety, rusty crane towered precariously, hanging from which was a huge metal weight suspended on a steel wire. We gazed in awe.

"No problem, Mrs Sheila" said Yiangos.

The idea of this invention is repeatedly to drop the weight on the same spot, thereby breaking up the ground, then, periodically, a large suction pipe is put in to withdraw the pieces of debris. Our two experts, suitably dressed in shorts and flip flops only, prepared to start it up. We took cover and watched from a safe distance. Amazingly, after a few false starts, it roared into action and the massive lump of metal thumped into the earth. All went famously for ten minutes or so and then the suspended weight came out of the perpendicular and the whole thing swayed and groaned alarmingly. With lightning agility and flip flops flying, one of the team leapt on to the gantry and caught hold of the steel wire, actually guiding it as it pounded up and down jerking him violently with it. As soon as the whole thing stopped swaying and the noise abated to its former steady racket, he leapt off, retrieved his flip flops, and stretched out nonchalantly once more in the shade of a carob tree.

After several hours of this unnerving procedure, the hose was put in again, the suction pump started and out gushed WATER! What a commotion, what excitement! It must have been like this in the first days of the Klondike gold rush. Word got round somehow and people began arriving to see this wonder. They came down from the village, from Polis and Argaka and Yialyia to marvel. The maestro told us that it was drinking water, they could tell from the strata in which it had been found. (Subsequent analysis proved this to be so). A shame to use it for the septic tank, so we instantly decided to keep this well for the garden and start again for the soak-away. Now came great ponderings and deliberations as to where to dig the second hole. We rejected most of these ideas (including one to site it well above the house and septic tank) and, faced with so much conflicting advice, Harry said to me "You decide, use your intuition, it doesn't often let you down".
All eyes turned to me in disbelief. They always knew the English were mad, he was actually going to let a woman make a monumental decision like that. Being of Celtic origin, with a Cornish grandmother and an Irish grandfather, I briefly considered getting a wire coat

hanger and having a go at dowsing, but my courage failed me in the face of so many disbelieving countenances. Pointing firmly to a spot I said in Greek, "We'll dig here".

"*OXI*", they roared as one.

It was definitely the wrong place, strata, whatever - all the signs pointed to failure. I remained resolute and, with much head shaking and muttering, the trusty machine was wired up again. They dug down fifteen feet, put in the hose and out gushed torrents of WATER - this time from a clay bed on the other side. Now the commotion could have been heard in Turkey. What a woman. In a dried-up valley, wherever she points they find water!

"Bravo, Mrs Sheila", said Yiangos.

"No problem, Yiangos" said I.

Weeks later the monstrous contraption was still there, stuck in a mess of mud and clay and now with a flat tyre as well. We stared at it gloomily, thoroughly convinced it would be there for posterity, standing amongst our future oleanders and hibiscus like some hideous ultra modern sculpture. We asked Yiangos if he could prevail upon the owners to remove it. He looked at the rusting heap, kicked the flat tyre, grinned broadly and said "no problem, Mrs Sheila".

Eventually the unsightly machine was taken away and the house gradually grew into a concrete shell, the supporting columns reinforced with strong steel rods as the earthquake regulations required. We then needed the skills of an expert plasterer, but were held up for some time as there were none available in this remote place. Then, one day, Nathanielis, a short, sturdy, decisive man, came to see us. He was a local builder, competent and much respected in the area. Covered in cement dust from the tip of the inevitable sun hat to the soles of his boots, he worked at a furious pace and woe betide any labourer who slacked on Nat's site. He did not suffer fools or layabouts. A glowing cigarette was a permanent fixture under the dust-powdered moustache and, beneath his gruff exterior, he had a tremendous sense of humour. We had come to know him well and, having heard that we were looking for a plasterer, he had brought with him a stranger, a small, wiry, fit looking man with a ready gap-toothed smile.

"This is Michaelis from Nicosia" he said "he's a very good plasterer and looking for work".

We took him on and he proved to be a swift and able operator. Dressed in faded shorts and flip flops, T shirt and battered cloth sun hat, which soon all became a uniform grey with plaster dust, he flung trowels full of the stuff, improvising precarious perches from planks, barrels and nailed-together bits of wood where necessary. He was as agile as a monkey and had no fear of heights.

He drove a wreck of a car and was lodging somewhere in Polis, having left his family in Nicosia. When it was time for the schools to close for the summer holidays, he asked for permission to bring his family down from the capital. They would camp in the shell of the house, he would not need anything apart from the things already there, and he would carry on working his normal daily hours. During this period it seemed that half the population of Nicosia was already here camping on the beaches and in the surrounding fields anyway, so we came to the conclusion that a few more wouldn't make much difference. Off he went and the following day his car came crawling up the track, virtually hidden beneath its load of foam rubber mattresses, blankets, pillows, suitcases, pots, pans, buckets and bowls and a basket of deep-sea fishing nets. Crammed inside was his plump little wife with their three children, who turned out to be not only bright and attractive but very well behaved.

In no time Eleni had sorted the place into a makeshift home and, with a small gas ring, concocted all kinds of marvellous meals for them. The children were kept spotlessly clean; she even had an old electric iron, with the cord cut off, which she placed on the gas ring to heat up and ironed their clothes every day.

Michaelis loved to fish and, with his eldest son, always brought something back from his late afternoon forays at the beach. Harry asked him one day how he managed to catch so many fish and he promptly invited him, together with our son who was staying here at the time, to join in that evening's expedition.

The four of them set off and, choosing an area near the Baths of Aphrodite that was not too deep, Michaelis and his son pulled a weighted net into a V-shape. The top of the net floated just beneath the surface and the bottom was held on the sea bed by the weights. According to Michaelis, it was going to make a big difference now that there were four of them instead of two. It soon became apparent why, because the object of the exercise was for the swimmers, wearing snorkel masks and flippers, to cruise around in the water and, when they saw a fish, chase after it and funnel it into the V of the net.

Needless to say, there was some scepticism on the part of the English team as to the feasibility of this method, but the Cypriot side was adamant that we'd all be stuffing ourselves with fish come nightfall. The four of them fanned out into a loose circle, Michaelis demonstrating once or twice, with wildly thrashing arms and legs and fierce grimacing, how to chase a tiddler or two into the net. After half an hour or so of this, my two were men-

They encountered a large shoal of sphyrnae.
Shoal of Sphyrnae.

tally planning a quick kebab sandwich for their supper when, unbelievably, they encountered a large shoal of *sphyrnae* and, with frantic flapping and gesticulating, herded dozens of them into their net. These fish are, in fact, small barracuda and, to me, they looked like a thinner, longer-snouted version of the mackerel I used to catch with my father and brother in Torbay.

That night, sitting under the stars, we all feasted together on these delicious fish, cooked to perfection over the glowing charcoal. Accompanied by fresh bread and salad and washed down with some of the local white wine, who, as the song says, could ask for anything more?

Michaelis' next project was to introduce us to another form of Cypriot cuisine and, accordingly, he asked if it would be all right to build an oven in the garden. His wife would make good use of it while they were here and we would have the benefit of it in the future. We readily agreed, provided him with the necessary materials and, in the space of a day, he built an oven with a square natural stone base and a domed top, like a beehive, which he lined with special firebrick. To preserve the ethnic look he covered the dome with *havara*, a pale local clay, mixed to a plaster with *acheron*, which is very finely chopped hay used as the staple winter food of donkeys, sheep and goats in Cyprus. There was a fairly big opening in the front of the dome and a small hole on one side, near the top, for smoke to escape.

A few days later he said "Tonight we are going to eat *kleftiko* so we will put it to cook before we finish work today".

The children were despatched to gather suitable brush and firewood and he soon had a big blaze going inside the oven. A large stone closed the opening while the fire heated up. Meanwhile, Eleni had prepared the *kleftiko* meat in its special earthenware pot, which had two handles, and a small lid. The chunks of leg of lamb were put in with onions, spices and fresh herbs (notably oregano) and the lid was sealed to the pot with a flour and water paste. In another pot she placed potatoes, with a little olive oil and seasoning, and sealed that up too. Her task was now completed, apart from preparing a large, fresh mixed salad.

Once the fuel had burned down to ashes, the stone was removed from the front opening and an enormous heat blasted out. The ashes were pushed to the sides and back of the oven and the *kleftiko* pots put in. Michaelis then placed the stone back in position and, with his expert trowel, slapped a mix of wet *havara* all round, sealing it completely.

"OK" he said "finished. Tonight when you come down, dinner will be ready".

Down we came at the appointed time, bringing the wine and two of the round loaves of freshly-baked village bread. A table made from a board, resting on some trestles and covered with a clean tablecloth, stood waiting with the plates and glasses, knives and forks and a huge bowl of superb Greek salad, the whole scene illuminated by a couple of hurricane lamps hanging in the carob trees. We gathered round as the maestro chipped away the clay seal and removed the stone. The *kleftiko* pots were carried to the table and, as they were unsealed, an unbelievably mouth-watering aroma filled the air. Soon we all had our plates heaped with succulent lamb, that fell off the bone, and the tastiest potatoes I have ever eaten.

Eleni reminded us of how this dish came to be named. *Kleftiko* comes from the Greek word *kleftis*, which today translates as 'thief'. The original *kleftis* were Greek Freedom Fighters trying to gain independence from the Turks. In the mountains of Greece they would avoid giving away their position, with the smoke from meat cooking on open fires, by placing their stolen lamb in sealed earthenware pots which they then buried in a hole filled with glowing ashes.

I took another mouthful of the tender meat and glanced down the table. The polished sheen of Mess silver, flowers and place settings seemed light years away and, somehow, obsolete. Harry caught my eye, raised his glass and smiled, and I knew with a shattering certainty that this was where we would finally put down roots. This would be our home for the rest of our lives.

CHAPTER 3

THE TOP OF THE WORLD

On days when there was a respite from work at the site, we took time off to explore the area we had made our home. The lack of proper roads did not worry us as we drove a strong, off-road vehicle which took us pretty well anywhere we wanted. In fact, we revelled in being alone in the grandeur and open space of the Akamas, passing only a shepherd now and then or a farmer from the village ploughing one of his outlying fields.

Our first explorations took us up through the village and along the track that passed the little church of Ayios Minas, wherein lies a stone which is said to have healing properties if passed over the affected part of a sick pilgrim. Set by a lovely natural spring which rose among a group of rocks, the water from this spring was crystalline in its clarity and there were always birds bathing and drinking, while huge grey rock lizards sunbathed on the boulders, completely immobile until an unsuspecting butterfly chanced to land. Then they would leap forward with lightning agility to grab and consume it. Well camouflaged against the grey stone, they looked like something straight out of the world of dinosaurs, particularly when seen through the macro lens of a good camera.

In January small scilla, like tiny bluebells, bloomed profusely among the rocks surrounding the spring; their delicate, sky blue colour breathtaking in its beauty. Later, at the foot of the tall pine trees which grew nearby and in the meadows below the church, many species of wild orchid appeared, some of them quite rare.

Further along the track another spring rose from a cave among an outcrop of big boulders in an area called Smyies. Here, in March, the ground beneath the pines was carpeted with the lilac pink of an orchid called morio libani, which bloomed together with dactylorhiza sulphurea, a lovely pale yellow one.

Past Smyies the track led up to a T-junction where, turning right, we could explore the northern side of the peninsula. At one high point we looked down over the curving bays and inlets leading to Fontana Amorosa and beyond, the pale creamy colour of the coastline disappearing into the turquoise and aquamarine depths of the sea. Near Fontana Amorosa an old shipwreck was evidence of the fierce gales that sometimes battered this northern shore and made local fishermen wary of rounding the point when the forecast was unfavourable. Today, still, when a really bad storm hits this area, as many as four or five large tankers may be seen sheltering in the lee of the cliffs. We always know the bad weather is passing when, one by one, they begin to pull out again.

If, at the T-junction, we turned left we looked out over the splendour of the southern coast. The ground swept away below us, thickly covered in pine and scrub, the only sound to be heard the sporadic bleating of wandering goats, their tinkling bells merging with the high, keening cries of large raptors passing overhead. The track led on down through shady pines to the sea and then along the coast to the turtle hatchery at Lara. Past Lara, towards Paphos, was the lovely little harbour of Ayios Georgios, with its own small island off shore. Here there were sea caves to explore and, nearby, was the magnificent Avgas gorge rising up through the mountain from below the village of Peyia.

At the very summit of the mountain, near the village of Droushia, was a place we called The Top of the World.

The original little church of Ayios Minas.
Ayios Minas.

From here, looking west, there was an uninterrupted view of the end of the island lying far below; the shape of the entire western coast and Cape Arnauti clearly defined as though seen from an aircraft. Around us were large outcrops of rocks where Griffon vultures reared their young and the air was balmy with the scent of broom. Intermittently, a dark shadow passed across the ground as one of these big birds soared overhead with upturned wingtips. Today, the Griffons have left this place, only the crags with the huge, white splashes of their droppings show where once they nested.

Between Droushia and the back of our own village of Neo Khorio the landscape remained much as it must have been in biblical times. Shepherds wandered with their flocks of long-tailed sheep among hectares of land dotted with olive and carob trees. An important crop for the village, the hard black pods of the carob were collected in August and September. Many of the fields were a long way from the village itself and the villagers travelled by donkey carrying large sheets, to spread on the ground beneath the trees, and very long, springy poles to knock the ripe carobs down. The familiar, rattling sound of the poles knocking and the pods raining down echoed around the whole area when it was time for the carobs to be harvested. Everyone in the family turned out to help and, once the carobs had been put into large hessian sacks and the tops had been sewn shut with string, they were loaded up on to the donkeys for the long trek back to the village. There the sacks were stacked in huge piles at a collecting point near the church, from whence they would be taken to the processing factory in Paphos. The sickly-sweet smell of carobs hung in the air and the women were busy with specially selected pods which they had reserved for their own use. The carob beans were washed and then smashed between two smooth pebbles before being put into a large cauldron of water over a wood fire and boiled into a thick, sweet syrup. Most of the crop went for pro-

Goats wandering on the Akamas.
Akamas goats.

cessing into animal feed, but the Health Food industry was becoming ever more interested as people in Europe became more health conscious. The fruit of the carob was sometimes known as St. John's bread, for it was said that when John the Baptist went into the wilderness and lived on locusts and wild honey, the locusts referred to were not the insects but the carob or locust beans.

No sooner had the carob crop been brought safely in than it was time for the olive harvest and the long journeys to the fields continued until well after the first rains. The olives were collected in large wicker baskets or plastic crates and, mostly, went to the co-operative mill to be pressed into pure, golden-green virgin oil or the thick, dark oil (made from olives that had been boiled up in the big cauldrons) for which our village was famous. We helped by dropping off loads of olives at the mill and returning with the containers of oil. Sometimes the jeep would be crammed with people all sitting on top of each other, glad to be able to avoid the long walk up the hill to the village with their heavy plastic containers. Meanwhile, the women were making *tsakistes*. The best green olives were washed and cracked between two stones before being put into a strong saline solution to keep. They tested the solution for its salt content before immersing the olives. When a fresh egg would float freely in it, it was ready. Once the jar was full, a fresh vine leaf was put over the top of the olives before it was sealed. Each year we were given enough olives and bottles of oil to never have need of buying any. Whenever we are given *tsakistes* we are also urged to take fresh garlic bulbs and crushed coriander seeds, for no self-respecting villager would eat his olives without first pouring over a little oil, crushed coriander seed and chopped garlic.

One of the nicest things we found about living in an isolated area like this was that everyone had relatives in the surrounding villages so that, wherever you went, you felt as though you were part of one big family. There were few foreigners and tourism had not begun to have an impact on this coast, so everyone knew us and invited us into their homes. Every wedding in the area became a huge social event, as family members from different villages were reunited for the day, and we were always warmly welcomed. We value the friendships we have made over the years and are now often attending the weddings of couples we first knew as small children in our village.

Latchi lies just below Neo Khorio and a couple of miles to the east is Polis Chrysochous, the centre of the region. The road running along the beach north-east of Polis passes through several small villages until it reaches Pomos and Pachyammos. Here, in order to get to the last Greek-Cypriot held village before the Turkish-occupied north of the island, the traveller had to make a long detour up around the mountain before descending into Kato Pyrgos, an attractive small fishing village. This detour was made to avoid the Turkish enclave at Kokkina. Hence the people of Kato and Pano Pyrgos were sandwiched between Turkish-held territory and, if they wished to get to Pomos and the free Greek area beyond, they were forced to add almost an hour to a journey that, were Kokkina not occupied, would take ten minutes or so along the coast road. This is a situation that still exists to this day.

On the landward side of this coast road was a fertile plain where fruit, mainly bananas and melons, and vegetables were grown. The terraced foothills of the mountains, leading up to Stavros-tis-Psokas, rose up from the plain, becoming more densely wooded with pine trees as they progressed. We would drive up into these mountains, marvelling at the sheer beauty of the scenery. Small dams conserved water for the villages below and it was a cool and shady place to collect pine cones and deadwood for winter fires. It was here that we had our first sight of the wild sheep which has now become the national emblem of Cyprus, the moufflon. We had stopped near one of the dams and were silently enjoying the peace and tranquillity of the place when, suddenly, no more than twenty metres or so away from us a female with a young one walked gently into a clearing. We were downwind of her so she did not spot us, and carried on picking her way daintily down the slope towards the water. Later, much further up in the forest, there was a flurry of movement and five young males, their heads crowned with curved horns, cantered across the track ahead of us. As soon as they saw us they burst into a full gallop and hurtled down the mountainside at breakneck speed.

These animals were some of those thriving outside the area fenced in by the Forestry Department at Stavros. There, in the large territory behind the wire, they lived and bred in their natural habitat and, as a bonus, had the benefit of a regular feeding programme. These swift, shy creatures were difficult to see, swerving sharply together and galloping away at speed as soon as they detected the presence of man. We always enjoyed our trips up through the beautiful Paphos forest to the Forestry Station and made a lot of friends among the officers there. They had an excellent nursery, growing young trees for the reafforestation scheme, and we brought back many sturdy specimens to plant on our land.

Back in the village we were never at a loss for advice on how things should be done, and everyone took a great interest in all we did. One of the things that gave me an instant rapport with the people with whom we came into daily contact was their pragmatic approach to life and, above all, their sense of humour. Every village had its 'character' - the one with the sharp wit who made everyone laugh. Ours was Lambis, by then in his seventies, but still alert and full of fun despite the inevitable slowing down as the years began to weigh more heavily on him. When he was in good form at the coffee-shop I could barely understand a word he said, which was probably just as well for I believe most of it was rather risqué to say the least. He was a legend in his own time; everyone knew of Lambis and his escapades. He loved to cock a snoot at authority. One day, while visiting someone in Polis, he tied his donkey to a tree outside the local police station. The beast took exception to being left there with nothing to graze on and set up a tremendous braying and wheezing. A village donkey in full voice is a force to be reckoned with; conversation in the near vicinity is impossible and, when Lambis returned, the long arm of the law came out to remonstrate with him for leaving it there and to enquire why the stupid, God-forsaken thing was making such a racket anyway. Lambis calmly unhitched his donkey.

"Well" he said, "his hopes were raised when I left him here and now he's crying because I won't let him join the police force".

Some seven or eight years later Lambis exited this world. He did it with his usual panache on Christmas Day and I am sure that somewhere still he makes even the angels laugh.

Our village was full of donkeys. A good working beast was worth three hundred pounds and the foals, which sold for about a hundred pounds apiece, were much sought after. People came from long distances to buy the animals, knowing that the Akamas donkeys were strong, healthy and hard working. Those who wanted to breed from their mares would take them up out of the village, as soon as they came into season, to be mated with the stallion kept by the shepherds. I remember one of our neighbours once asking if he could come with me into Polis when I went shopping the next day. He would be outside our house at half past seven all ready to go - At seven o'clock he passed the house riding one of his donkeys in the opposite direction. "Are you not coming to town with me?" I asked.

"Can't" he replied "My donkey has to go to Androulikou to get married".

We grew to love these long-eared, noisy animals who were an essential part of village life, but little knew that, before long, two particular donkeys would play such a large part in our own lives.

And so the long summer days passed in working and exploring the territory while we learned about and bonded with the people. Bright images flow through my mind of what everyday life was like then.

Tiny ox calves and donkey foals, all long legs and big eyes, galloping through the village street or playing alongside their working mothers; and the mad panic as they scrambled for safety under their flanks when something startled them.

Dinos' gentle monotones from behind the wooden plough as he coaxed and guided his two big, black oxen around the steep field adjacent to our site; and the booming, penetrating voice of Theodoulos as he ploughed one of his fields with two grey donkeys hitched to the plough.

The women, with the morning chores completed, sitting together in groups, their work-worn hands busy with delicate and beautiful crochet work as they talked.

The smell of fresh bread baked in the big outdoor ovens and cooling on platters of woven straw.

Games of Tric-Trac in the coffee shop when I went to collect the mail. The anticipatory grins as the men

He coaxed and guided his two big, black oxen.
Oxen Ploughing.

asked how many 'no problems' we had encountered that day, and the laughter as I stumbled my way through colloquial village Greek.

The day Orania's pig escaped and the speed and skill with which the pink blob managed to evade capture. Orania, red and panting, as she hotly pursued it round the garden wielding a brushwood broom with a style and grace that would have done credit to Severianos Ballesteros. Her angry shrieks turning to helpless laughter as I joined in the frantic chase, eventually cornering the culprit in a small shed; and the expression on her face when she opened the door to see the pig crammed up against the wall with its forelegs splayed out over the white china splendour of her newly-installed toilet.

Welcoming hands and smiling faces in a sea of black shawls as the older women made way for me in church, each wanting to hold my hand and stroke my arm; and their touching devoutness as they prostrated themselves during parts of the service, those too stiff and arthritic to get right down on to the floor holding tightly to the pews and bowing their heads as low as they could.

Ptolemos, the shepherd, and his granddaughter at sunset one evening, passing us on the narrow track up through the pines to his mantra; the donkeys steadily picking their own way across the rough ground as their riders each cradled three or four new-born kids in their arms. The sound of bells and the plaintive bleating of the she-goats echoing through the trees as they followed closely behind.

And something that made me put all my problems in perspective and never failed to calm me. The awe-inspiring beauty of the view out over the Akamas from the Top of the World.

CHAPTER 4

DRAMAS WITH DONKEYS

While building was progressing we had a steady stream of friends and colleagues to visit from the British Base at Akrotiri. They came to commiserate with or envy us, depending on their outlook. One day we received an urgent message to contact a Squadron Leader who was also an avid horseman. The stables at Akrotiri had a pet donkey. Donk for short, his 'pedigree' name was DON QUIXOTE! A great favourite with the children, he was getting on in years but was even-tempered and in good health. We learned that a new army vet had been posted in and would not allow a donkey to be stabled with the horses. Poor old Donk was about to be ousted.

"You've got plenty of room for him up there and there are loads of other donkeys already" they pleaded "besides, you can ride him up and down to your land every day".

It was only when we had agreed to have him that they told us he would need a stable companion - he was not used to being on his own. Oh well...... One of Theodosis' donkeys had just foaled and the baby was a pale, creamy, beige-coloured female with limpid eyes that would have melted a glacier. I fell in love with her at first sight and she was mine, instantly christened Sheila, of course. What else?

Faced now with the prospect of becoming donkey owners, the day dawned when it was decided that I should learn to ride one. If I was going to keep them, I was going to have to be able to ride them. I wasn't too sure about this idea; now that my daughter had elevated me to the rank of grandmother, somehow it didn't seem quite dignified. A brief silence greeted this observation, followed by "since when have you ever been dignified?" Having no suitable answer to this, I foolishly agreed to start by riding up to the *vrisi* with Theodosis, when he went to water his animals in the evening.

Theodosis was a tall, upright man with a wicked sense of humour. Father of five, with several grandchildren and a few great-grandchildren, he was still very much the head of his family. His Greek ancestry showed in his good looks and green eyes, one of which he had lost in an accident some years previously. His physical workload was phenomenal for a man of his age. He could lift sacks of carobs, weighing fifty kilos or more, with comparative ease and climbed trees to a terrifying height when it was time for the olives to be harvested. In order to reach some of his far-flung fields, he would have two or three hours travelling by donkey, every-thing he needed having to be loaded up on to the beasts each time he made the journey.

For those who think riding a donkey is easy, I would point out that this is nothing like riding a tame little beast along the beach at Weston-Super-Mare, with the donkey walking in a straight line over nice, level, soft sand. For a start, here you are riding over rough, rocky and extremely hard terrain and these things have a mind of their own. The only command they seem to be given is "Brree-O" together with lots of unintelligible curses which I assume are Greek, but which could equally as well be Outer Mongolian to my uninitiated ear. Instead of a leather saddle the Cyprus donkey has a thickly padded cloth, on top of which sits a wooden saddle, shaped to curve over the animal's back. All man-ner of paraphernalia is attached to this and the donkey is generally ridden side saddle by men and women alike, although some men do ride astride.

One of Theodosis' donkeys had just foaled.
Theodosis.

Standing next to the saddled donkey it appeared to be as big as the side of a house, and about as easy to get on. Theodosis, who is well into his seventies, placed one hand on a stout stick and vaulted, from a standing start, to land, with a plop, squarely in the middle of the wooden perch. I elected to stand on a chair first so that I could glide gracefully across, but the donkey had other ideas and kept ambling away, leaving me stranded in the middle of the field standing on a red plastic chair. Harry watched this charade with some disgust.

"You are" he said witheringly "a teacher of physical education. Are you telling me that you are not athletic enough to leap up that little distance?"

"OK then, let's see you do it" I snapped somewhat waspishly.

So he did, just as my mount moved off again and he landed in a heap on the floor. This improved my sense of self-worthiness no end and, eventually, while he held on to its head collar, I scrambled aboard. I do not care for heights and from up there the ground looked a frighteningly long way down; but my donkey was getting thirsty and, as soon as Theodosis went "Brree-O" and moved off on his mount, mine made a mad dash for the track to follow it. This was when I discovered that these things do not respond to whoa, WHOA, STOP, or HELP! Clinging on for dear life, I was jolted up the road to the *vrisi*, with every bone in my body jarring against the next and my teeth clenched to avoid severing my tongue. We passed all four coffee shops, to great hilarity and ribald comment, until we came to the *vrisi*. This was near the church and, to get to the water, a short, but steep, cobbled road, which had about a 1 in 4 gradient, had to be negotiated. This, being slippery and wet with all the water already spilled, did not seem to me to be a suitable place to pursue the art of donkey-riding for the first time. My donkey, however, did not care a fig

How I could ever have agreed to keeping donkeys...
Working Donkey.

for this, he could smell the water and he went for it, sliding down, with his hindquarters almost touching the ground, and coming to a sudden halt at the bottom, neatly shedding me in the process. Relieved to find I was still alive and did not require major surgery, I bathed my face in the cool water, picked up the reins, and led the treacherous beast all the way back.

"You'll never learn to control the thing like that" said my spouse "I'll give you a hand with him tomorrow".

Tomorrow dawned and I waited until the donkey had been watered before venturing forth again. Theodosis poured himself an ouzo and watched with interest from the shade of the mulberry tree. This time, decided Harry, we would both get on and sit astride the beast. I would be sure to feel more secure with someone sitting behind me. I probably would have had it been with anyone but him - I should have known better. As soon as we were both firmly squashed in the saddle, he spurred the donkey to a fast trot around the field and, terrified, I saw we were heading straight for a tree which had a low branch sticking out sideways.

"DUCK" I yelled and laid my head down over the massive ears. Harry, true to form, grabbed hold of the branch and stayed there hanging on it while the donkey, now relieved of his weight, cantered even faster round the field until Theodosis, who should be canonized, got up and brought it to a halt.

How I could ever have agreed to keeping donkeys after this amazes me - my brain must have been affected by the jolting, but Donk duly arrived in a horse box towed behind a Landrover and, as soon as she was old enough to leave her mother, Sheila moved in too.

Donk whiled away his days in retirement eating lush grass and dozing in the shade. He ambled amicably wherever led and did not make half the noise the local beasts made. The baby donkey adored him and he basked in this admiration, putting up with her skittish playfulness with remarkably good humour. Harry built a stable in the back garden, Theodoulos obligingly moving his donkey to another old house he owned nearby. Sheila followed us around like a pet dog. We took her for long walks and she would canter away, only to come galloping back along the track giving us a flying 'monkey jump' sideways as she passed. All the baby donkeys did this to their mothers in play and it was quite endearing when she was small but, as she grew, believe me, half a ton of donkey flying through the air at you is no joke. I think she guessed I didn't enjoy this game so much and she became very cunning. She would dash off ahead and lie in wait behind some suitable cover, leaping out at me from behind as I passed. We became extremely attached to these animals and our association with both ended sadly.

Donk somehow, somewhere, ate some foliage that had been treated with pesticide (at least that was the vet's guess). He became listless, would not eat and was obviously in pain. The government vet arrived with his assistant and, when they got over their amusement at someone keeping a donkey just for fun, they were marvellous. They looked him over thoroughly, then showed us how to pour a bottle of oil down his throat, using a stick to keep his teeth apart. Then they gave him an injection with an enormous syringe and left, leaving us with instructions to give him the next injection early in the morning. The following day Donk looked really ill. He was still standing and Harry was next to him, with his arms around him, shouting to me to hurry up with the injection. I struggled with the syringe (which looked like something you might use for cavity wall insulation) and, when I went out into the garden, I saw Donk slowly keel over - only Harry's quick reaction saved him from being pinned underneath. That was it. There we were with a ton of dead donkey in the garden and temperatures rising in excess of thirty degrees Celsius. I spoke with the *Mukhtar* who smiled, when he saw there were tears in my eyes for something of such little account as an ass, but he was ready to help, as always, and, within half an hour, Savvas arrived with his tractor and Donk was taken away. We were upset for weeks.

Sheila continued to grow into a magnificent beast but a major snag arose when I learned I had to go into hospital. I would not be able to handle her and look after her properly and Harry needed all the time he could get coping with the building programme. Reluctantly, we looked for a new home for her. After turning down several would-be owners, whom we did not feel were genuine animal lovers, we eventually let her go to an old farmer, called Sofranos, who had several big orchards of citrus fruit. Her job would be to move along under the trees carrying the big wicker baskets of oranges and lemons.

Harry got ready to walk all the way to Prodhromi with her.

"She'll never go off with him without me" he said.

Old Sofranos slipped a head collar over her head and turned.

"Brree-O" he said, and she walked demurely away behind him without giving us a second glance.

As the weather warmed up we were not enamoured by the smell from the drains, such as they were, so Harry decided to clean all the areas in under the metal covers next to the house. He opened them up and, with gallons of Jeyes fluid and a hosepipe, flushed them all through. "Great" we said to each other "that's more hygienic".

We also liked the residual smell of the disinfectant, which is more than the original inhabitants of the drains did. That night, in bed, I said "what on earth is that noise?"

"I was just about to ask you that" replied Harry, who had also been lying awake listening to the sound, which was a bit like brown paper crackling. He got up, switched on the light and we froze in horror. Because of the lack of space, the bed had been pushed up against the wall and the whole of the wall was now a seething mass of cockroaches, presumably disturbed from the drains. My instinct was to flee, but I was rooted to the spot by the graceful athleticism of Harry, naked and with a flip-flop in each hand, as he leapt and bounced on the bed, swatting cockroaches off the wall and swearing like the proverbial trooper at the same time. This man's versatility never ceases to amaze me.

The weeks passed and storm clouds began to roll in over the mountains. Before long, lightning flashed, thunder rumbled and rain began to fall. When you live here you welcome the first rains; the parched earth soaks it up and people are reassured as the dams start to fill. It was coming down heavily so we retired inside, only to find it was almost as wet in there with water pouring through cracks in the flat roof. We hastily moved furniture around and placed strategic buckets and bowls. It rained for days and the weather turned rather cold. There was, by then, only one dry place in the house - at the back of the hall, so we pushed the bed in there. We lit a log fire to cheer ourselves up, but had to sit by it with each of us holding an umbrella. I felt cold, wet and so ridiculous I didn't know whether to laugh or cry. Harry, always a positive thinker, jumped up.

"I'll put on some music" he said "what'll it be, Mahler or Beethoven?"

"How about Handel's Water Music" I said, and we sat by the fire, under our umbrellas, shaking with hysterical laughter.

The festive season approached and we were inundated with invitations to various neighbours' homes as they observed the annual preparations for Christmas and the New Year. The traditional bread was baked in the stone-built outdoor ovens and the time drew near for the slaughter of the family pig. The poor beast is pampered, cosseted and overfed all year then, in December, just when it thinks it's got it made, along comes the hand that fed it and slits its throat.

One of our neighbours, Sophocles, a swarthy, wiry and excitable man, with a luxuriant moustache and a large family, cordially invited us to witness the ceremony. He was scathing of the modern day namby-pambies who did not observe this yearly ritual. There was nothing to it if you were well-organized. He assured us he was very well-organized and, furthermore, he had taken even greater care this year not to let the pig know what was coming for, understandably, it might get upset and not walk willingly to its destruction. "Somehow" he said, sharpening a knife that looked long enough to run an elephant through, "they always seem to know".

We sat on a wall in the sunshine and watched as a trestle table was set up in the courtyard and a huge copper cauldron filled with water and put to boil over an open fire. The village priest was summoned and arrived, with all his regalia, to bless the ceremony. We never did find out if this was to absolve the pig-stickers from any blame or to make sure the pig didn't die in sin. The stage was set for the pig's opening.

Nothing would be wasted - the liver, kidneys and other choice titbits would be cooked, as soon as the job was

The pig trumped his ace.
A pig.

finished, and eaten by the menfolk, seated around a long table, while the women continued with the processing of the pork (a sight guaranteed to convert one instantly to total vegetarianism).

With a great show of nonchalance, in order not to alert the intended victim, Sophocles, and one of his sons, sauntered casually into the field opposite the house to fetch the pig. The huge porker, having been tethered by the hind leg all year, gorging itself and increasing its girth, now showed its intelligence by taking off before the death squad reached it. Muttering and cursing, the two chased resolutely after it, but it kept eluding them by tweaking the trailing rope away just as one or the other was about to grasp it. Sophocles sent for reinforcements. His wife, two more sons and three daughters joined in the chase. The pig, realizing it was outnumbered, set up a high-pitched squealing and, with eight people all shrieking simultaneous instructions to each other as they charged around the field, the noise was deafening. Eventually, one of them grabbed the rope and, with the fugitive bagged, the women returned to the house, leaving the four men to bring home the bacon.

The pig dug its trotters into the earth and refused to budge. They heaved and strained and cursed and kicked but they couldn't move it an inch. Sophocles got a short, sharp stick and poked the pig in a rather tender part of its anatomy. The pig retaliated by squirting a jet of evil-smelling, green, liquid manure up his arm. An enraged Sophocles, moustache quivering with indignation, rained curses and blows upon the pig, which suddenly took off again, dragging the youngest son, who was clinging to the rope, after it. It reached the road in front of the house and, pressing its enormous posterior against the wall, dug its heels in and would not be moved. Sophocles played his ace. The pig hates dogs, so he unleashed his hunting hound to nip at the recalcitrant heels. The pig trumped his ace. It lay down in the road so that the dog, faced with an amorphous mountain of blubber instead of a nippable set of legs, quickly lost interest and disappeared. This was the final straw. Sophocles, swallowing his pride, appealed to some of the pigless namby-pambies for help and, with a few more burly men and some extra rope, the massive bulk, still protesting shrilly, was dragged past us to the place of execution. At this point my courage failed me and, suddenly remembering an urgent chore I had left undone, I fled, almost tripping over my spouse who had, just as suddenly, remembered he needed some more film for his camera.

We returned, after the squealing had stopped and the river of blood had ceased to flow down the prepared channel, and Harry bravely sat and clinked glasses with the victorious men, while I duly admired the dexterity with which the women sliced and scraped and cut and thrust, flinging various portions of unidentifiable flesh into a cauldron of boiling water.

Parts of that pig seemed to last forever. For months strings of *loukanika* and chunks of *lounza* were pegged on the washing line in the sun, to be taken indoors and hung on a cord, stretched above the fireplace, whenever it rained.

Meanwhile, next year's piglet lifted its dripping snout from the stone trough in the field and watched the house, the cunning little eyes not missing a thing as it, no doubt, planned its strategy for the last-ditch battle that was to come.

The following spring there was a continual coming and going of relatives and neighbours as they began preparations for a wedding next door. The garden was cleaned up, the walls of the house whitewashed and the whole place swept from top to bottom. The women were preparing food for days and, as the big day drew near, a huge copper cauldron was placed over a wood fire in the garden and the traditional *Rezzi* was brewed up. This is cracked wheat, with lots of fatty pork and lamb, slowly cooked until the meat falls off the bones, which are then removed. It is cooked and stirred until the end result is a glutinous, porridge-like substance in which the wooden spoon will stand up. No village wedding would be complete without this great delicacy. Huge trays of minced meat with macaroni were prepared together with *kleftiko* meat, potatoes and salads.

On the great day the village barber came to shave the groom before his *koumpari* dressed him in his wedding suit. In another room the bride, a lovely dark – eyed girl, was being made up and dressed in her elaborate wedding gown by her attendants. While this was going on the older women brought the bridal mattress outside to be blessed by the village priest, before small crosses, made from red ribbon, were stitched on to each corner. Then, to ensure that the first born child of the union would be a male, a loudly-protesting small boy was rolled across the mattress and, as the violinist played, the women picked up the mattress and danced it round the courtyard. The mothers of the happy couple then came out with clean sheets which they folded into a cross over the mattress, dancing it round once more, before throwing on to it a few ten pound notes. The hint was duly taken and, as the fiddler continued to play, all the other relatives in turn approached and made their fiscal contributions. When the money had been safely stowed away the mattress was, once more, hoisted aloft and everyone took turns in getting underneath to dance it around until, at last, it was taken indoors.

In the late afternoon, when the church bell began to ring the fiddler led the way as the bridegroom, holding hands with his father and with all his *koumpari* around him, began his walk through the village street to the church. The bride, accompanied by her attendants and preceded by two children, carrying large be-ribboned candles, and a little girl, carrying a tray with the circlets, which would be placed on the bridal pair's heads during the ceremony, walked along the street with everyone craning their necks to see and admire her beautiful dress. All this tradition was heady stuff to us and the air was charged with excitement, gaiety and expectancy.

The wedding ceremony itself was a very crowded and noisy affair, which appeared to take place in utter chaos, but, wed at last, the happy couple returned to the house, where they lined up with their parents to receive congratulations from everyone, and each guest was given some sugared almonds, prettily wrapped in a twist of tulle tied with gold thread. Later the feasting and celebrating got under way in earnest, with masses of food and drink being consumed.Then gradually, the dancing began. The fiddler fiddled away furiously, fortified by the local brandy and turning alarmingly red in the face. The bride and groom got up together and began to perform a very Arabic, swaying dance and everyone, beginning with the parents and close relatives, came and pinned money to their clothes; some of the bridal attendants holding pincushions to provide the pins. Soon the newly – wedded pair were covered in streamers of one, five and ten pound notes.

The older men, now with quite a few toasts under their belts, were beginning to show their paces on the dance floor, vying with each other to see who could still show the most athletic prowess. The highlight of the evening, for me, was when some of the young bloods joined in and they performed Zorba's dance - each one trying to see the others off the floor as the music got faster and faster.

There must have been a few aching joints, not to mention heads, the next day, but no one knows how to throw a party like these hospitable, fun-loving people.

CHAPTER 5

AN AWESOME SIGHT

The weeks passed and we saw our house growing before our eyes while we adjusted to the way of life in the village and the different pace of things. *Siga, Siga*, slowly, slowly, was repeated dozens of times a day. Whatever you were doing, rushing at it would get you nowhere. *Siga, siga* was the way to do it.

We became used to the very early rising of the population. Not like Englishmen and mad dogs - they start work in the cool and, when the sun blisters down at mid-day, take a siesta until it cools down a little at four o'clock, when shops reopen and life begins to bustle once more. Sometimes the early mornings in the village were rather noisy. We had become accustomed to the donkeys and cockerels but, during August, a man used to arrive daily in a battered van at 5 a.m., pressing the car's horn every few metres and bawling through a loudhailer, which was attached to the roof, *"Echo batihes"*.

Harry, not even having had his first cup of tea, would mutter darkly "I don't know what a *'batiha'* is, but, when I find one, I'm going to stuff it down his throat" (or words to that effect, I think he said 'down his throat'). Later we learned that *'batiha'* is a Turkish Cypriot colloquialism for water melon, so it was really rather fortunate that Harry never managed to catch up with him.

One day a man called Costas, whom we had previously met a few times, drew up outside the house in a pick-up

They take a siesta.
Villager.

truck driven by a stranger. In the back of the truck were two *pitharia*, massive earthenware jars, used in the villages for storing oil or wine. It needed three or four men to lift the unwieldy things and they were much sought after by Cypriots, who earthed them up and used them as ready made ovens, and by hotel owners, who wanted them for display purposes.

At the bottom of our garden there was a wall, which was the same height as the back of the truck, and Costas wanted to roll the *pitharia* off into the garden so that the stranger could get back to his village before dark. Harry duly helped with the off loading and Costas, trying to agree a price with the other man, turned to me and said "I only need one of these for an oven, but he is insisting on seventy pounds for the two. Do you want one for thirty five pounds?" I'll say we did! Not easy to come by, and costing at least a hundred pounds when they could be found, we accepted the offer with alacrity. Costas duly got his jar moved and ours sat there for ages, awaiting the right opportunity to be taken down to our new house.

This opportunity came one day in the guise of three visiting RAF officers. They had hitched a ride out to Cyprus on a near-empty aircraft and had come up to the village to see us. They would be sleeping on mattresses on the floor that night. Fortified with a few bottles of the local brew, and with Harry acting as Flight Commander, these four Squadron Leaders with the little mini moke, a few planks of wood and all the cushions and sacks of straw they could find to act as padding, transported the huge vessel down the bumpy lane to our new garden. It rolled down the planks and off the moke to the accompaniment of roars of laughter as one or the other of them was bowled over by the weight. How it ever got here in one piece will always remain a mystery to me, but, today, it still stands beside the house with the pink trailing geraniums cascading from it almost hiding the date which had been scratched there, with a little drawing, by the children of the man who made it in 1887.

Christmas came and went and visitors continued to show up. An old friend, David, was staying with us and we introduced him to our friends and neighbours in the village. One day we were sitting in Theodosis' kitchen, passing the time of day and drinking tiny cups of the local coffee. David and Theodosis, each unable to understand a word the other was saying, were smiling and nodding amicably at each other when a yard cat had the temerity to enter the house. Mine host placed his boot under the scrawny creature's stomach and, drawing back his leg, flung it high in the air to land, screeching, among the hens outside. David watched this dispassionately over the rim of his cup.

"Animal lover are you, Theodosis?" he enquired.

On one of the first warm evenings we were sitting outside, enjoying the moonlight and listening to the soft calling of the Scops owls, when I noticed something fly into a tree in the next garden. It looked like a big owl, but it was black. Standing up to investigate, we ducked instinctively as a huge bat swooped low over our heads and landed in a *mespilia* tree. It grabbed some fruit and flew off to hang upside down from the electricity wires to consume it. This was our first introduction to the flying foxes, or fruit bats, which the local people call *niktokorakos*. They live in caves in a big gorge behind the village and stream out at night to feed on soft fruit and grapes. David Attenborough was later to come here to film them for his TV series THE FIRST EDEN. He identified them as Egyptian fruit bats, descendants of those reaching here from Africa when the Mediterranean was a dry basin. Fruit bats normally roost in trees and, with their large eyes, are able to see at night to collect fruit and return to the trees. Here, in Cyprus, the winters are too cold for them to stay permanently outside, so they have adapted to living in deep caves and, to enable them to find their way in the total darkness inside, alongside their sight, they have developed a radar system similar to that of other bats.

Some time after the filming Harry and I went, with one of the original guides for the film crew, on an expedition to the caves to photograph the bats. We set off in a jeep, driving up out of the village along a muddy, pitted track, shaded with aromatic pines and leading through acres of land covered with olive and carob trees, until we came to the end of a steep ravine, where grey boulders, worn smooth by the torrents of rushing water in an earlier age, would soon be clothed in the glorious pink of flowering oleander. Here, we ran out of road and bumped over rough ground, sometimes skirting fields that had been planted with *krithari*, the barley that was to feed the donkeys, sheep and goats. At last we reached a plateau of short, dry grass and scrub, which was covered with anemones as far as the eye could see. Pale rocks gleamed amongst the colours of the flowers and in the shelter of prickly shrubs, where they were protected from the ravages of the goats, wild orchids bloomed. A squadron of jackdaws flew past and a kestrel hung in the air, waiting for exactly the right moment to drop like a stone on its prey. We were now at the very edge of the gorge and, looking back, the village was like a picture postcard, with the pale-walled, red-roofed houses clustering round the church and straggling down towards the coast. The mountain behind the village sloped down to the sea which, on this clear, warm day with no heat haze to distort the vision, was such a vivid blue it looked almost unreal. The fields were still green from the winter rains and, with the anemones and bright yellow, scented broom flowering beneath the scattered carob trees, it was a sight to lift the spirit and gladden the heart. Whistling, and the

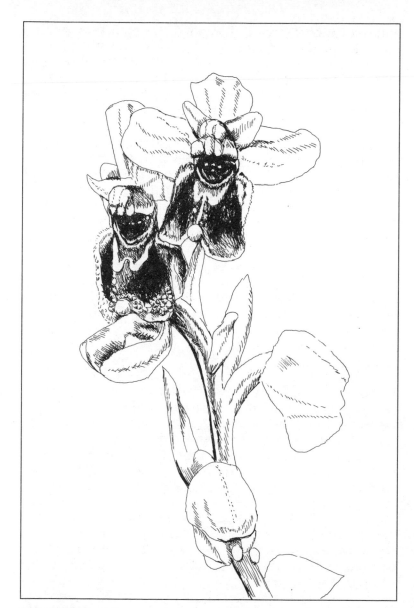

Wild orchids bloomed.
Wild Orchid.

sound of bells tinkling, heralded the arrival of a huge flock of sheep and goats, spilling out on to the plateau to feed now that milking time was over. The shepherd was our neighbour, who stayed most of the time in a nearby cave tending his livestock. We exchanged greetings and news and then turned towards our goal.

"Be careful here" warned our guide and, as he moved ahead, we came upon a large fissure, running parallel to the edge of the chasm, down which the unwary might easily disappear. The side of the gorge appeared to drop steeply away and, at first sight, it seemed impossible there could be a way down. Then Andreas indicated a narrow 'chimney' in the rock and I followed him, as he led the way, with Harry bringing up the rear. We had to ease our shoulders through the narrow gap, one at a time, and then we were on a hidden goat trail leading down the steep sides to the bottom of the gorge. A trickle of water flowed towards the sea and, here, the grass was lush and green. Glad of our leather boots and thick trousers, in case of snakes, we crossed the water and started the climb up the other side. About halfway up the trail, before the sides became sheer rockface, Andreas stopped and clambered over a large boulder, disappearing down into a narrow opening. We followed closely behind and, suddenly, found ourselves in a big cave with the ceiling high above our heads. We could hear whisperings and flutterings and squeakings and, as our eyes became accustomed to the dark, we could make out the interior walls going back a long way in places. We directed the beam of a powerful floodlight upwards and hundreds of fruit bats, huge eyes dominating their furry faces, were hanging there in groups above us, those we had disturbed crawling over the rockface, others detaching themselves to fly across and hang in another place.

With the floodlight extinguished it was very eerie in the cave - a weak shaft of sunlight, from an opening high up

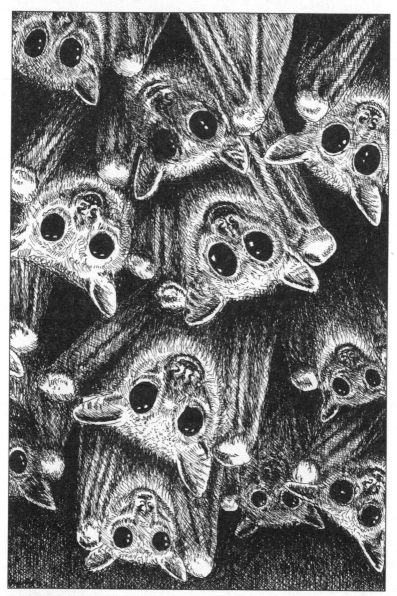

Huge eyes dominating their furry faces.
Egyptian Fruit Bats.

on one side, adding a ghostly glow. I stood there in awe, savouring the moment, aware of how privileged we were to be able to witness and record this rare and remarkable sight. The feeling was to stay with me for a long time afterwards and, even today, I am unable to see one of these flying foxes land in a fruit tree, or take water from the pool, without recalling the timeless scene in the cave.

The following summer, the young son of some friends at Akrotiri was staying with us for a few days. He was desperately keen to see the fruit bats, so he and I set off one evening to stake out an apricot orchard at Latchi. We saw hares, hedgehogs and hawkmoths, a rat, a fox, some tree frogs and lots of owls, but no fruit bats. By ten-thirty we were becoming disheartened and I knew that James must be very disappointed.

"Come on" I said "let's go down to the beach and see if we can find a turtle".

Over the years we had spent many days and nights in the turtle hatchery at Lara, where the Department of Fisheries has an ongoing programme to save the endangered green turtle, Chelonia Mydas. Patrolling the secluded beaches there to tag the turtles, that come ashore in the dead of night, is an exciting, exhilarating and rewarding experience. After trudging to and fro over difficult terrain, sometimes for hours, it is impossible to describe the emotion when, under a star-encrusted sky with moonlight silvering the sun-warmed sand, this big, primaeval creature emerges silently from the sea. It is an awesome sight that leaves me filled with wonder.

Turtles need deserted, sandy beaches to lay their eggs and our beach was certainly that. It was a beautiful, calm night with a full moon. We left the jeep at the top

Soon she began to lay.
Breeding Turtle.

of the cliff and walked down to the water's edge by the white rocks that give the place its name, Asprokremma. Keeping close to the water line, we began to walk towards the far end of the bay and, after a hundred metres or so, I saw one set of tracks in the sand. With experience it is possible to tell whether the tracks have been made by a loggerhead or a green turtle, and this track was, unmistakably, that of a big green. With mounting excitement we ascertained that there was no second track leading back into the sea and I knew she was at the top of the beach to lay. I whispered to James to keep close behind me and, dropping face down on to the sand, we began to crawl on our elbows, Indian fashion, up beside the track, which showed up clearly in the moonlight like the marks made by a huge tractor wheel. Soon I heard the sound I was expecting, the rhythmic 'swish' of sand being thrown. She was digging! She had almost finished the large excavation with her big front flippers and was down inside, with the moonlight glinting on her carapace. Every now and then we could hear her rasping breath. She edged forward and, with her rear flippers, began to dig the deeper hole where she would deposit her eggs. First the right flipper, curved into a spoon shape, and then the left; lifting out the damp sand and pressing it firmly until she had her nest ready. She moved forward and lay motionless, her egg depositor over the hole. Soon she began to lay - the spherical, leathery eggs (rather like ping pong balls) dropping one by one into the nest. She would not stop now until she had finished. From time to time she raised her head, huge tears forming and trickling from her eyes as she laboured on. We counted the eggs as they fell, one hundred and five in all. Spent, she stayed where she was, slowly recovering, then began to push the damp sand in over the eggs. Once she was satisfied, she moved forward and began to throw dry sand backwards with her front flippers until the nest was completely covered. Now, even with the tracks to guide you to the nest site, it would take some expertise to locate the actual hole containing the eggs. Her task over, she was eager to return to the safety of the sea. Much lighter and with a downhill route, she dragged herself to the water's edge. The first wave lapped over her, washing away the dried sand, and her beautiful markings showed clearly in the moonlight. Another wave surged silently over her and she was gone.

Later that summer, one hot September afternoon, I was walking along the beach with a small boy from the village. We were looking at various beautifully coloured stones and we found some unusual shells and a dried-out starfish. I showed him the tracks of a big turtle and then we saw the miniature ones made by the hatchlings where they had scrambled down to the sea. I asked him if he thought he could trace the imprints back to the nest and perhaps we would find some of the egg shells left in there. He was fascinated to learn that the baby turtles had come from eggs buried under the sand and had managed to climb out by themselves. Carefully following the tiny tracks back to their source, he excitedly indicated where he thought the nest was hidden and we knelt down and began to scoop away the sand. I soon located the nest hole and, as I lifted out the remaining sand and exposed the broken egg shells, there, at the very bottom of the nest, was a lone, struggling loggerhead hatchling, unable to climb the steep sides without the benefit of the others to clamber over. I gently picked it up and placed it in the palm of my hand, where it immediately turned to face the sea. (In the hatchery at Lara, when the hatchlings surface and are contained by the safety cages over the nest, they will always crowd on the side nearest the sea). It was very hot now and I knew it would have a better chance of survival if we released it after dark, so, giving the baby turtle to the child to hold, I placed some damp sand from the nest in his sun hat and we put the hatchling in. He carried it, oh so gently and carefully back to the car and then home, where we put it in a bowl and waited for darkness to fall.

At about eight o'clock the moon began to rise and we set off for the beach with our little charge. We put it on the sand, a few metres below the nest site, and it immediately started scrambling for the sea. We followed it down the beach until it reached the wet sand, where a gentle wave washed over it and its small body was sucked out in the undertow. Swimming strongly, it headed out to sea while the child and I stood, hand in hand, and watched it go. I knelt and put my arms around him as I heard him sob at the little creature's going.

"Don't cry" I said, "he'll be safe now that he's reached the sea", but my own heart ached for his sadness and the loneliness of the tiny turtle on its hazardous journey.

I hugged him close for a moment and then we heard the herons calling. Looking up we saw lines of them, strung out against the moon, flying steadily overhead. His tears forgotten, in his delight at seeing this new wonder, he skipped along the sand, full of the things he had to tell and the wonderful drawing he would make tomorrow. Our spirits lifted by the sight of the birds winging their way south, we made our way up the beach and home to bed.

CHAPTER 6

FOWL PLAY!

At last we moved into our new home. We had no electricity or telephone but we were in! It was a marvellous feeling sitting on the front verandah by candlelight that night, watching the moon rise over the mountains. At first, the scene below us was enhanced only by starlight and the twinkling lights of the villages around the shores of Chrysochous Bay to the point at Pomos; then the mountains were backlit by a warm glow and the perfect, orange sphere of the rising moon appeared above the peaks, creating a golden path across the sea towards us. As it rose higher in the sky the light paled and the shape of the bay was revealed, gleaming like beaten silver.

Suddenly, the silence was broken by the rolling bark of a dog fox close to the house. We looked up and there he stood, silently sniffing the air, in a gap between the cypress trees which were on a level with the verandah. He stayed there in the moonlight for some moments, head raised and pointing towards the village, before moving on like a shadow. Someone was going to be short of a hen or a pigeon come morning. Bats flitted by our flickering candle and owls called softly now and then. The only other sound was the prreep-ing of tree frogs. A moment later we realized we were not alone - a small owl was sitting on the balcony rail looking at us. It appeared to be quite unperturbed by our presence and, after several characteristic sideways movements of its head, took off, as suddenly as it had appeared, and glided down into the garden. As it went I heard it call quite clearly.

"It's a Johnny" I said with some excitement.

It was our first close encounter with a Scops owl.

The next morning we were awake before daybreak and, too elated at being in our new environment to lie in bed, we were up in the living room, drinking the first welcome cup of tea of the day, as dawn broke and the sky glowed deeply red, slowly lightening to a warm rose, shot with gold, and suffused with crimson where mist still wreathed the mountain peaks. Warm rays flooded the verandah and the water in the bay danced and sparkled in the early morning breeze, changing, from a rosy opalescence to clear blue, as the sun rose higher in the sky and burned away the last vestiges of mist and cloud.

We breakfasted on the verandah in the warm sunshine, savouring the sights and sounds around us. I noticed a large slow-worm on the marble tiles; it was quite dead, and certainly had not been there the previous day. We puzzled over this, but came to no convincing conclusion. During the course of the day, armed with binoculars, I found myself on the verandah, at every possible break in our work, looking at a variety of birds. Among them I recognized pied wheatears, goldfinches, greenfinches, a spotted flycatcher, Spanish sparrows and a woodchat shrike, not to mention many others I could not positively identify. I even saw a magpie with a moustache! Tethered in a field in front of the house was a large grey donkey and, perched on its back, was a magpie carefully pulling out another long hair from the docile beast's mane to add to the bunch it already held in its beak.

"I wish we had a birdbath" I said.

By lunchtime, having carved out a shallow stone bath, Harry was cementing it on to a pedestal he had made from three blocks of stone pegged together. By teatime we had filled it to overflowing with water and retired, binoculars at the ready, to the verandah above. A male blackcap was quickly in the water, creating a tremendous splash - often totally immersing himself. Cyprus warblers, a Sardinian warbler, with his bright red eye ring, and the little black and white pied wheatears who, together with the Scops owls, were to become our permanent guests and remain our firm favourites, all came to drink and bathe. As dusk fell, I kept hearing a faint purring sound, like a kitten, but a search revealed nothing. During the evening we saw the owl several times, landing on the balcony rail and taking off again. Sometimes, as it glided down into the garden, it would give a loud "wheeow", which we assumed was a warning cry.

Loud as it was, it was nothing compared with the shrieking of the Little owl that followed soon afterwards. The cry was piercing and prolonged and rose to a wailing crescendo. Here, these birds are known as *kukufiow* - a name of onomatopoeic excellence, and the villagers, who are, in general, superstitious about owls and, in particular, about this one, claim that every time you hear one shriek someone in the vicinity dies. They must have been dropping like flies in the village as we sat there that night.

We have some friends, who bought an old house for a holiday home in the nearby village of Droushia. When they went home, they left instructions for a fireplace to be installed so they could spend winter holidays here. Returning to Cyprus the following Easter their night flight arrived at Larnaca airport and they hired a taxi to bring them on the long journey to Droushia, cordially inviting the taxi driver in for a cup of coffee before he set off on the return trip. Opening the back door,they were dismayed to find two dead owls in the kitchen. They had obviously discovered the new chimney and, in investigating this likely-looking nest hole, fallen down through and been unable to find their way out again. When he set eyes on the little corpses, the driver hurriedly crossed himself. "These are devil birds" he said and, swiftly declining the offer of a welcome cup of coffee, could not scramble back into his vehicle quickly enough and leave.

Because we had no electricity, in the kitchen we had a small refrigerator which operated with bottled gas. It sat on a kitchen worktop with a beer crate stowed underneath and, to prevent the possibility of fumes collecting in the kitchen, the trapdoor, leading to the roof-space immediately above the fridge, was left open. I went to get a drink of cold juice later that night and was startled by a grey shape which appeared to lunge at me. Harry fetched a torch and there, perched on the edge of the beer crate, was a fluffy, silver-grey baby Scops owl, his enormous yellow eyes staring defiantly at us.

We now realized why the adult bird kept landing on the balcony rail and why the slow worm had so mysteriously appeared - the owls had to be nesting in the roof space. Thankfully, the tiles over the front verandah had not yet had the facing boards put up. The fledgling must have been trying out his wings and fluttered across the roof cavity, dropping down through the open trapdoor into the kitchen. I picked him up gently and he glared at me. Harry stood on a chair under a beam at the end of the verandah and I handed the fledgling up, at which point he began to shriek. What an incredible noise he made! You would have thought we were trying to strangle him. This commotion brought the agitated parents in and they swooped and dive bombed us as we tried to get him back up near the nest. Once his feet were firmly on the cross beam, he shuffled around, until he was facing us again, and glared as if to say "how DARE you". He dropped in regularly after that and became quite accustomed to being put back up on the beam, at least

I was easily able to find them roosting in the carob trees.
Scops Owl.

he never made as much noise again; he rather suffered the imposition in disdainful silence, although we always got the haughty glare. There were a further two chicks in the nest and, when the adult birds arrived or called, they made this purring sound I had heard so many times before. Shortly afterwards all three fledglings fluttered on to the verandah and were last seen gliding down into the garden with the adult birds in close attendance.

When we came to put up the facing boards and close in the roof space, we put below it a false ceiling of trellis, through which some of the bougainvillea could be trailed and, high in one corner where they had nested, we put an owl box. We guessed at the size, from having seen the birds at close quarters, and kept the design simple.

The following February they began calling near the house and, by day, I was easily able to find them roosting in the carob trees. As the weeks passed they drew closer together as they slept during the day and, at night, they started landing on the box every now and then. In April they made more frequent visits and their calls became louder and more ringing. Towards the end of April we heard a lot of scrabbling and scraping in the box and one morning, when I slid open the big verandah windows, an owl jumped out on to the ledge of the box and stared at me. The idea had worked.

They have remained permanent lodgers and we have become very attached to them. They are excellent parents - the female remaining in the box with the chicks until they are almost ready to fly. The male is never far away and, throughout the day, they keep in constant touch with each other. As the fledglings grow and demand more food, they will sometimes hunt during daylight hours. One very hot day, when the female was sitting on the ledge of the box getting some air, her mate silently appeared on the verandah and landed on the back of a chair with a small, soft-bodied lizard dangling from his beak.

Now in May some years later, as I type this account, the same box still sits above my head and I can hear the female turning her eggs and softly answering her mate, who is roosting in the carob tree opposite.

We had a lot of land to turn into garden and, slowly, it was beginning to take shape. Where the ground was too hard and rocky to grow shrubs or trees, we found big stones and turned it into a rockery. There were hundreds of rocks and stones lying around for the taking, some of them extremely beautiful, either in shape, texture or colour, sometimes all three. Some 'honeycombed' ones picked up near our land are pieces of sea coral. Others, formed in a long-ago age, have layered strata of pink and white and grey and green and have been worn smooth by the sea.

The garden terraces were planted mainly with geraniums, pelargoniums and flowering shrubs: scarlet, orange and white hibiscus, blue plumbago, multi-coloured lantana (producing the sweet, black berries the birds love so much), red, pink and white oleander, aromatic lavender and rosemary and Daphne, giving us fresh bay leaves for the kitchen. Red and purple bougainvilleas climb the walls of the house and the delicate, sweetly-scented, white flowers of the stephanotis cling round the bathroom windows. We grew 'walls' of oleander around the car port and planted a climbing vignonia to clothe the uprights with its heavy clusters of brilliant yellow blooms in October. Our aim has been to plant those flowers and shrubs which thrive in the hot sun and require the minimum amount of water; and also to have something in flower at all times of the year. From December, wild cyclamen, for which this area is famous, flower all over the garden and, later, the rockeries come alive with pink, white and yellow alyssum and *matsikoritha*. Soon the air is filled with the heady perfume of freesias, which have seeded themselves amongst the flowers and shrubs, and, in April, the stone walls of the terraces are ablaze with *metaxakia* which open in the sun, showing their beautiful faces in pale pink, lilac, deep purple and dark red. In earthenware pots, of varying shapes and sizes, we planted trailing geraniums and petunias, and old stone sinks are filled with verbena and begonias. Night-scented jasmine clings to the side wall of the studio and honeysuckle twines around trellises near the house. Wherever possible we planted trees. Oranges, lemons, figs and pomegranates, apricots, nectarines, peaches and plums, lotus fruit and mangoes were all lovingly put in. We even planted a *mespilia* down by the stream bed for the fruit bats! In one corner of the small orchard I planted a beautiful jacaranda tree in memory of my mother. She died more than twelve years ago, but I miss her still and the glorious blue flowers of the jacaranda tree appear around the time of her birthday.

Harry dug a patch of ground for vegetables and planted tomatoes, peppers, aubergines, lettuce, cucumbers and radishes and we enjoyed being self-sufficient in salads.

Thankfully the garden has matured and flourished, despite the scarcity of water in the first couple of years and the ravages of our chickens before we managed to get everything permanently fenced in. When the pool was under construction and the fence was down again to allow access to the heavy machinery, it even survived the daily trampling and rooting of several half-grown pigs, belonging to a woman who seemed incapable of keeping these porcine pillagers confined for any length of time. Now the only problem is trying to find the time to do all the watering, dead-heading and pruning and, of course, the interminable weeding.

One day Giorgos, from the coffee shop, who is also the Postmaster General of the village, asked me if I would stop at the vet's office when I went in to Polis and bring him back a box of day-old chicks. At the office I was filled with euphoria. I told the vet how sweet the little yellow balls of fluff were and he persuaded me to take a box too. I thought how nice it would be to throw them a handful of corn now and then. After years of globe-trotting with the Royal Air Force, we had our first permanent home and we were really in to this self-sufficiency business. Wouldn't it be marvellous to have our own supply of free range eggs? What he failed to tell me is that there are two kinds of day-old chicks - those which grow up into very large (and extremely stupid) white hens, good for the table but not much good at producing eggs, and those which grow up into small, brown hens that become prolific layers.

Giorgos' box had twelve chicks, which all grew up brown and gave him lots of eggs. My box had thirty chicks, which all grew up white and gave us lots of headaches. For a start, thirty balls of fluff don't take up much room, but, after a few weeks, we were wading through hordes of voracious chickens who would have made a shark feeding frenzy look like a picnic. Harry had to fence in a piece of land with chicken wire and then construct a wooden hen house, complete with perches for them to roost on. We gave these misfits names for quick and easy identification. There was Waddle, with some kind of congenital leg deformity and Dumbo, with some kind of congenital brain deformity (they probably had her in mind when they coined the term 'birdbrain'). Kipper Feet kept tripping over everything in sight and always managed to fall off the perch - she was the last one out of the hen house in the mornings, having spent the night fluffed into a nest of straw at the back. Some names, born out of descriptive desperation, I cannot reveal here because of the Obscene Publications Act. We had to buy their food by the sackful and stuff for this or that impending ailment to put in their drinking water. Then, of course, they had to be cleaned out each day. The toil was never ending.

The day eventually came when they were big enough to be eaten, so we decided to reduce our numbers and, at the same time, have delicious, home-grown, corn-fed chicken to eat.

"How are you going to kill them?" I asked.

"What do you mean, how am I going to kill them, that's women's work in the village, you do it".

I recalled my horror at the sight of knives flashing and headless chickens running round the garden (they really, truly do).

"No way, not a chance" I said.

"OK, I suppose I'll have to do the dirty work, as usual, but I'm not using a knife".

We discussed various ways of murdering our victims, including drowning, strangulation and hitting them over the head with a blunt instrument, then I stayed inside while Harry strode purposefully out to the chicken run. A terrible commotion ensued with panic-stricken squawking and flapping wings. Eventually all went quiet and I ventured out to see my husband leaving the enclosure with a large cardboard box under his arm.

"How did you do it" I asked.

They assured us we needed a cockerel.
The Wimp.

"I didn't" he replied "I've got two of the blighters in here and I'm taking them up to the village to ask Theodosis to do it".

We never did eat any of our hens. How do you tuck in to roast Waddle or curried Dumbo when you've known them so well? Chrissy, Theodosis' wife, although never quite being able to understand why, would gracefully accept the cardboard box containing one of our birds and, opening the fridge, would give me one of theirs all ready for the oven. Sometimes it would be IN the oven and I'd take it home hot and tasty and ready to eat.

When we were down to about a dozen hens, Nathanielis came to build an art studio for Harry. He and his handsome son, Dinos, were highly amused at our chicken set-up.

"Where's the cockerel?" they asked.

They assured us we needed a cockerel to keep the hens in order. He would marshall them, protect them and, in general, keep them in their place. In return for his favours they would lay us more eggs. We did not have a cockerel, partly because we couldn't stand the thought of one starting up down here once all the others in the village began crowing before dawn, but also because the local cockerels, as we well knew, were pre-eminently disposed to be fierce and aggressive.

Nat and Dinos decided to play a trick on Harry and they smuggled a young cockerel into the hen house before he went out the next morning to release the hens.

"They're making a hell of a racket in there this morning" he said as he went out.

When he let down the door, the cockerel, who was supposed to be marshalling his hens and keeping them in good order, streaked out, absolutely terrified, with the indignant hens, who were all at least twice his size, in hot pursuit, pecking at him until they drew blood. He cowered in a corner, a pathetic sight, only half-grown and scrawny with it. He was instantly christened the Wimp. I picked him up and got some corn and he soon began to peck feebly at a few grains. We had to isolate him, however, and for ages he would only eat from my hand because he knew I was there to protect him from the belligerent hens.

He was, on this preferential treatment, to grow into a fine bird with magnificent colouring and a crow you could have heard on Mount Olympus and boy, did he get his own back on those hens. When the time came, I think most of them were glad to get into the cardboard box.

Eventually the Wimp was boxed up too but, by then, their cockerel being considered a bit past it and ours being such a fine specimen, Theodosis kept him to rule the roost at his place.

One day we were working in the garden as usual when down the lane came Theodoulos with his donkey train. Built like an ox, a man of immense physical strength and an almost childlike naïveté, a bellow from Theodoulos could shatter the eardrums at ten paces, and all conversation was conducted at top speed, with spittle spraying, until he was forced to a strangled halt in order to draw breath. He owned a lot of land and had four or five grey donkeys. You could hear Theodoulos coming long before his straggling procession of donkeys came into view. They would be roped together, one behind the other, and a baby one would usually be gambolling alongside as they set off for his fields. He and his wife had no children and I once asked him why he didn't sell some of his land and live a life of luxury in the South of France. He pondered on this question for a while and then said "but what would I do without my donkeys?" Today, a bright orange, wide-brimmed, ladies' cloth sun hat shielded him from the glare of the sun and a constant rumble of inconsequential Greek came from him as he coaxed, encouraged or cursed his donkeys. We waited for the usual barrage of greetings he would fling our way as he passed, but were quite unprepared for the commotion that followed. So was he, judging from the strength of comment he made as the donkey shied up and deposited him in the roadway. "*Kyrie Elyson*", he roared, scrambling to his feet and striding over to our gate. "Quickly, please bring me a drink of water".

He was standing, holding the trembling donkey, and was visibly shaken himself when I returned with the glass of water. The donkey had narrowly missed treading on the dreaded *koufi,* the bluntnose viper. He indicated that it was about a metre long and as thick as his arm, which was notably brawny and muscular. This snake is the only really dangerous one in Cyprus and the local people fear it. Our valley, with its stream-bed and natural spring rising lower down, was an ideal habitat for them.

After this incident I decided that I would try and learn as much as I could about snakes, from a knowledgeable source rather than from superstitions and old wives' tales. I had heard about an Austrian herpetologist, married to a Cypriot and living in Paphos, whom the local people knew must be mad because he actually liked snakes and urged them not to kill them. It was time to make contact with him, and so Snake George came into our lives.

They would be roped together.
Theodoulos' donkeys.

CHAPTER 7

SNAKES ALIVE!

Snake George's knowledge of English was a bit flawed here and there, but he certainly knew his stuff when it came to the herpetofauna of Cyprus. Dressed always in unassuming khaki fatigues, he was a quietly-spoken man with a shock of reddish-brown hair and fair skin, which turned a fiery red in the sun. Snakes were his passion. He had studied them in the field in far-flung countries and he regularly exchanged information and views with various Institutes around the world.

Firstly he showed us how to recognize each of the eight varieties of snakes that exist in Cyprus (until recently there had been thought to be only seven, but George had discovered a grass snake, that had never been recorded, and made it eight). He explained their habits and how to cope should an emergency arise. He would arrive at our house on his motor bike and, from various bags and pockets, sometimes even stuffed inside his shirt, he would retrieve a snake or two to show us. In order to protect the snake, it would have been put inside a piece of tubular gauze, or, failing that, one of his wife's nylons with the top tied in a knot. I used to have visions of the poor woman opening her dressing-table drawer to find only one-legged pairs of tights inside. Time was of no essence to George when he was dealing with snakes and, by the time he arrived at our house, he was invariably hours late and still had about an hour's journey to get to his home. The Cyprus Telecommunications Authority had installed a radio telephone for us and he would telephone his long-suffering spouse who, with two small daughters to care for, could not leave until he got home and was probably already late for her shift at the local hospital, where she was a much-respected midwife. He would hold the cackling telephone away from his ear while she berated him and, every now and then, would interject placatingly with "yes, my sunshine, no, my sunshine".

He treated the bluntnose viper (Lebatina lebatina) with great respect and showed Harry, who was forever collecting rocks and stones for landscaping, how to roll the rock back towards him, so that his lower legs were protected in the event of one being asleep underneath. The snake's instinct is to go away from you, as quickly as possible, unless you corner it or tread too near it when it is asleep, in which case it will almost certainly strike. He brought a smallish specimen to the house one day (thankfully in a box and not tucked inside his shirt) and, tipping it out on to the ground, held its neck down to immobilize it before picking it up behind the head. Even this small one had vicious-looking fangs and I was glad when it went back into the box and didn't escape into the garden.

From time to time we had seen a black snake in the garden. It was a large whip snake (Coluber jugularis), a species growing to twelve or fifteen feet in length. Quite harmless, it was a very fast-moving snake and George told us that, in addition to rats, mice, birds and lizards, it ate the young of the viper. Moreover, being territorial, if this one stayed in the garden we would be unlikely to get any of the poisonous ones moving in. So Oscar stayed, and is still with us, although he is now more than two metres long.

George, who gave lectures in schools around the island, asked if I would make a film for him. The idea was to show someone fairly incompetent, gaily tripping through the undergrowth in flip-flops and Cyprus sun hat, exposing himself to all kinds of reptilian reprisals, (he suggested Harry for this part, much to his disgust). Then he, Snake George, would enter left, wearing all the right gear, and show how to correctly handle a snake. To this end we prepared a site, opposite the house, by putting in several piles of prickly bush for him to 'search' under and, beneath one, we planted a snake. It was a coin snake (Coluber nummifer) beautifully marked and about two metres long. This snake, although harmless, is fast becoming another endangered species, because it has the misfortune to closely resemble the venomous bluntnose viper and is usually killed on sight.

I set the camera up on a tripod.

"Roll 'em" I yelled, in true Hollywood fashion, and into view came Snake George 'walking in nature', as he put it, and wearing all the appropriate apparel for one about to mess with snakes. He eventually got to the right bush and lifted it up.

"Ah" he said knowledgeably, "Coluber nummifer".

He picked it up and the snake promptly wound itself round his arm, opened a surprisingly large mouth, and bit him on the finger.

"Yee-oow" yelled George, desperately trying to dislodge it. I zoomed in on the snake's head and could clearly see the blood trickling down. The mouth opened and let go of the finger, only to immediately grab it again and give it another mangling. George was coming towards me for help in removing it and, to my eternal shame, I carried on filming because it was so fascinating. Harry, having heard the shout, came out and the snake was removed. The fingers needed bathing with antiseptic and George needed a cup of coffee and a stiff brandy before we prepared to film his next snake, which was an exceptional find. The

Institute in Bonn had said there was evidence of the existence of an indigenous species of snake called Coluber cypriensis. Related to the black whip snake, it was small and slim and had some white markings on its, otherwise, black skin. No one had previously discovered a live one to prove that they really did exist, until George, on one of his regular field trips up in the Troodos mountains, saw one drinking from a pool of water in the road and managed to capture it. He now had the only one of its kind in captivity in the whole world, as the snake is to be found nowhere but Cyprus.

So with half an hour to spare, while the intrepid film star recovered, I set off for nearby Polis in the jeep, which had the hood rolled up for the summer. I went to pick up a video recorder that was in for repair and parked outside the workshop so the engineer could easily lift it in. When I arrived he was just finishing work on it so the vehicle was left, open and unattended, for a while before he loaded the box in the back and I set off home. I was about halfway there, at Latchi, when I saw a frantic Snake George tearing towards me on his motor bike like Barry Sheene. He threw the bike down on to the beach and rushed over, to where I had stopped, shouting "my snake, my snake". I had no idea what he was talking about - I thought perhaps the snakebite had affected his brain. He dashed around to the back of the car and wailed in despair when he saw the big box inside.

"My cypriensis" he moaned, "I wanted her to be safe while we were filming, so I put her in the back of the jeep in the shade".

I sat there frozen with horror. I had just been all the way to Polis carrying a snake, which was the only one of its kind in captivity; open to the assault of any stray cat or dog, not to mention Machos shoving a great big box in on top of it. George, hardly daring to look, pulled the box forward and there, coiled peacefully in the regulation stocking, was cypriensis. She was perfectly unharmed, thank God, but he was taking no chances now and slipped her inside his shirt before retrieving his bike, and, with the dedication that befitted a true performer, followed me back to the house to finish the rest of the filming.

The next time I had occasion to film for Snake George was when he wanted to collect some vipers, for his exhibition, from the far side of the big ravine behind the village. Harry drove the Pajero with me, holding all the camera equipment, in the front and Snake George in the back with a box suitable for harbouring venomous snakes. When we reached the gorge, we selected a site, not far from the track, which, George considered, would have snakes in plenty. The box was set down on the ground and we fixed the camera on a tripod in a small space between the bushes, where I could zoom in all directions if necessary. I tucked my trousers firmly into my leather snake boots and prepared to do my bit. In the distance, spread out all over the sides of the gorge, in a peaceful, pastoral scene, we could see a huge flock of sheep and goats grazing. George told us he was inclined to be wary of the shepherd, with whom he had clashed on previous occasions, for, like most local people, he hated snakes and maintained that they should all be killed on sight.

Climbing down the sides of the gorge towards the water, George then worked his way up towards us, ferreting around under rocks and bushes and probing in various crevices with his special stick, trying to flush out a viper. Suddenly, he and Harry both shouted at the same time, and, before I could react, they told me one had just gone into the bushes, near my feet, where it had disappeared. He carried on searching and another one slithered towards me and secreted itself under the loose rocks - there wasn't even time to focus on it.

"Can't you slow them up a bit, George?" I asked, keeping the camera focussed on the end of his snake stick. This time a medium-sized one made its way out from another opening of the crevice he was poking about in, so I missed that too, but Harry assured me it had joined the others in my vicinity. I was knee-deep in the things by now and we had not captured so much as a glimpse of one on film. By then the light was fading fast and George, who was desperately hacking around in the undergrowth by my feet trying to discover the fugitives, had just pinned one down by the neck with his stick when, with a swirl of dust, a battered pick-up truck braked to a halt and a large, red-faced individual got out demanding to know what was going on. This, of course, was the shepherd George had been so apprehensive about - and I could see why. He was of gargantuan proportions and his demeanour was decidedly hostile. George blanched and dropped his camouflaged hat on the snake, in a pathetic attempt to hide it, knowing the man would certainly kill it if he saw it. I smiled at the shepherd and told him we were making a film to warn tourists and others of the dangers they might face in encountering snakes in remote areas like this. Moreover, we intended to remove one or two of the worst kind to put in the exhibition at Skoulli, so that people visiting there would have a chance to see and recognize them. The custodian of the flock appeared to be satisfied and, mollified at the thought of a few less in his area, he very nearly smiled as he backed up the truck and roared off.

No sooner had he gone, and George had the snake firmly grasped behind the head, than another cloud of dust heralded the arrival of a tourist Z-car and a friendly English couple, having seen the camera equipment, stopped, curious to see what was going on. The man got out of the driver's side and his wife rolled down the window nearest to us. Snake George, ever keen to initiate the unenlightened into the delights of herpetology, said "haf you efer seen a poisonous snake?" and, wishing them to get a better view, held the thing, with its triangular fangs exposed, close to the window of the car. He might just as well have said "ve haf vays of making you talk" because the window whizzed up and the man dived into the car, showing an unexpected agility for one his size, and, with a nasty grating of the gearbox, the car shot off down the track. I'm willing to bet they didn't stop until they reached Larnaca airport.

Hans-Jorg Wiedl, Snake George, was later to be honoured for his project on the herpetofauna of Cyprus. He was given an honourable mention (and a very expensive watch) in the Rolex Awards for Enterprise 1993. These awards are given every three years to only a few scientists worldwide, so it was a very considerable and well-deserved achievement.

Spring was really in the air and birds were collecting nesting material all around us. The Spanish sparrows had decided to colonize the bougainvilleas, which covered two sides of the house up to the roof. The one on the front verandah was a prolific grower and a glorious bright purple, while the one on the rear balcony was a magnificent red. Altogether there must have been more than thirty nests and they proved to be rather noisy, for the male Spanish sparrow selects the nest site and begins to build, stopping every now and then to utter his, piercingly loud, "cheep, cheep, cheep" to attract a mate. When a female shows up to have a look he tries everything, short of actually standing on his head, to woo her. He is a real showman and, as well as doing most of the building, he does more than his share of bringing food for the chicks when they hatch. Despite the noise, I like having one of these little show-offs a few feet away from the kitchen window, and many a dish

The Spanish sparrows had decided to colonize the bougainvilleas.
Spanish sparrow.

has been left unwashed as I gaze admiringly at their frenetic performances.

The problem is that we are unable to protect them from the plundering of Oscar, the big black whip snake in the garden. He unerringly knows where and when to find nests full of plump baby birds. One day, when all the nests had hatched and there was tremendous activity as the parents flew to and fro with food, we heard a commotion that far outdid anything we had previously heard. Dashing outside, we saw dozens of Spanish sparrows fluttering and swooping and shrieking at the top of the bougainvillea on the rear balcony. The shrub was not fully in flower and the nests could be seen quite clearly; so could Oscar, who was actually coiled up inside one having already eaten its tiny occupants. From there he could put his head into the adjoining nests and vacuum up his next meal, coiling himself inside (all two metres plus of him) until he was ready to eat again. Harry fetched a long pole and we managed to dislodge him. I was able to get some good video of the controlled way he came down the sheer walls of the house, but there was no way we could stop him from going back, and this he did, time and again, until he had devoured the lot. We tried pruning the bougainvilleas back hard so there would be nowhere for the birds to nest and they would be forced into some of the hundreds of trees that surround us here, but one persistent little character, whom we call Franco, managed to find a spot strong enough to work on this year and he built a nest and successfully attracted a mate. His was the only one up there but, as soon as the young birds had had time to fatten up a bit, we heard the dreaded commotion again. Franco received all kinds of support, from other Spanish and house sparrows, but to no avail. Oscar was already at the nest by the time we arrived and we were too late to save the fledglings.

I am not sure if it is Oscar or not (Oscar could very well be a misnomer, for I have no idea whether he is a male

Every now and then they did a kind of dance.
Snakes Mating.

or a female) but, one day, we were coming back from an early morning swim and had just turned the jeep off the road, on to the track that leads to our house, when we saw an incredible sight. Harry, who was driving, stopped the car and we stayed there, captivated, watching two black snakes, each about two metres long, mating. They were coiled and entwined around each other and were weaving their heads closely to and fro. Every now and then they did a kind of dance, almost standing up on their tails. This vertical position was so unusual and so beautiful that we were cursing the fact that we had neither video camera nor Harry's photographic equipment to record it with. We did have in the car, however, my small idiot-proof camera, which, when aimed at the subject and pressed, will automatically focus and rewind by itself. I leapt out and started to take a few pictures and Harry, who was still sitting in the jeep, said "That's no good, you'll have to get a lot nearer with that small camera", so I shuffled up the track a little further. They were in the middle of the lane, still oblivious, although, normally, the car would have sent them streaking for cover.

"NO, get nearer to them" he hissed in an urgent whisper, so I moved still closer, and, with my eye glued to the viewfinder, pressed the button until the film was used up. Lowering the camera, I visibly jumped to find I was practically standing on top of them. We watched them until they slowly subsided to the floor and, just as slowly, began to glide towards the stone wall. Again I had the feeling I have had so many times, living in this beautiful and largely undeveloped area, that of being extremely privileged to witness something rare and, for the most part, unseen.

Oscar remains, for the most part, unseen but turns up in the garden, from time to time, usually when we have someone visiting who is terrified of snakes, when he will obligingly put in an appearance. He seems to have a great sense of timing. Once we had some keen bird watchers on the front verandah observing a family of goldfinches splashing and drinking from the birdbath below us. One almost-grown fledgling was happily paddling about in the overflow beneath the pedestal when Oscar's head appeared from under a nearby lantana bush, and, before we could do anything, he grabbed the youngster and promptly ate it.

Sorry as I am at the fate of his victims, Oscar, too, has his place in the ecological pattern and is, himself, a thing of beauty as he pours his gleaming ebony coils over the rockery and disappears among the flowers.

CHAPTER 8

KINGFISHER BAY

Not long after we had arrived in the village to live we had become friendly with a family of sponge fishermen, and they introduced us to the true beauty of the coast around us. They had a marvellous old wooden boat, painted bright green, with TAPPAS DIVERS proudly displayed on the side. Michaelis, although by no means old, had been diving a long time and had suffered from the bends more than once. As a result he had a slight limp and doctors had warned him not to dive again. He was now forced to rely more on his sons. Dighenis, the eldest and most adventurous, was sponge-diver-in-chief and the good-natured, curly-haired Charalambous assisted him. The third son, old enough to participate, was Giorgos, a handsome, gentle boy, loved by everyone.

Taking a picnic basket and sun umbrella with us, we would meet up with them in the early mornings and the noble old boat would chug steadily out of the tiny harbour at Latchi, hugging the coast, towards Cape Arnauti. I loved those early mornings when the sun was not yet too fierce and the sea was calm and crystal clear, its colour changing from a glorious blue to darkest indigo over the deeper parts and to an incredible turquoise where we passed over white sand and rocks. Often we would see turtles swimming in the depths below us, the clarity of the water affording every opportunity to tell whether they were loggerheads or green. Other fishing boats would pass us coming back from bringing in their nets, the fishermen already beginning to check the night's haul, and greetings echoed across the intervening space as we passed each other.

They had a marvellous old wooden boat.
Tappas Divers' Boat.

The scenery became ever more beautiful as we progressed. Steep-sided slopes, clad in dark green trees, swept down to an uninhabited and largely inaccessible shoreline on our left, while, on our right, was the small island of St. George, where seagulls nested in the spring and herons and egrets rested during their autumn migration. We passed a small bay, with a sandy beach, that was good for swimming. It could be reached by road, but not with an ordinary car, for the road was almost non-existent and pitted with large holes and rocks. Not far after this there was another small bay. This one had no beach at all but was surrounded by smooth white rocks, and, at the back, there was a big sea cave. The water here was very deep and it was a superb place for snorkeling. Shortly afterwards we reached the bay where we would stop. It was fairly wide with an island in the middle, the water becoming shallow as a small beach was approached. The rippled sand beneath was pure white and the sea a clear, jewelled turquoise. It was like a tropical desert island, only the palm trees were missing. We called this paradise KING-FISHER BAY, because two of these beautiful birds nested there. It was always a joy to watch the bright flash of colour as they streaked across the bay to perch on the rocks, repeatedly diving for the small fish that abounded there. This bird has the Greek name Alkione and the village women told me how it came to be named.

Alkione was a beautiful girl with whom the God, Zeus, fell in love. His jealous wife, Hera, turned her into a small bird, destined to lay its eggs in February, when the weather would be cold and the sea rough. The other Gods on Olympus, taking pity on her, created a two week period of calm weather to enable her to build a nest and, from her name, we get the Halcyon Days, the period of calm during the winter months beloved of fishermen.

Michaelis brought the boat in and we disembarked, wading ashore through the warm water. The boat turned and chugged off to where the divers would be collecting sponges. They would be calling for us on their way back in the afternoon.

It always rather amazed me that they survived to pick us up again, for to say that the boat was not too well organized and equipped was an unparalleled under-statement. The line, through which the diver's air passed when he was down in the depths, was piled hap-hazardly all over the deck, with baskets of fishing nets and containers for the sponges stacked on top, the crew trampling, unconcernedly, over this vital lifeline as they walked to and fro.

Not so very long ago, Mediterranean sponge divers used to go down in a spherical glass helmet attached to a heavy leather smock which fitted over the body. An air hose was screwed into this and the helmet and smock were filled up with air. Once the diver was down on the sea bed, he was kept supplied with air by means of an ancient pair of hand-bellows operat-ed by someone on board. There was a slight snag with this system, however, in that the diver had to remain in an upright position. If he tripped and fell over when he was walking along the sea bed, or tilted over too far when he bent to collect the sponges, the air inside the suit was displaced and sea water flowed in to replace it, causing the unfortunate diver some considerable dis-comfort.

This 'old fashioned' method had been discarded by our divers and they went down on the 'modern' Agila line. They dived to depths of up to fifty metres simply dressed in swimming trunks and snorkel masks. A con-tainer for the sponges was tied to a belt around the waist by a rope which led up to the boat. When the con-tainer was full, a firm tug on the rope indicated to those aboard that it was to be hauled up. Strapped to one leg was a big knife for harvesting the sponges, and the end of the airline, which had been coiled so untidily all over the deck, was fitted with a demand valve then looped around the diver's chest and secured with bits of old string. This way, if he dropped his vital air supply, it would remain attached to him and could easily be recovered. His life-sustaining air came down through the line from a small compressor on board. Of course, there was no back-up system if this should fail, but, fortunately, it never did, although, once or twice, the boat swung round in the wind and diesel fumes from the compressor were sent down the line to the hapless diver, necessitating his rather sudden return to the surface. It gave you palpitations to see this system in operation, but they always did come back, and with loads of beautiful sponges too.

The rest of the equipment was somewhat sparse. There were no lifebelts, liferafts or lifejackets, and, once, I recall sitting in the bows, with my feet clear of the debris, as one of them flung out the anchor. I was idly watching the rope uncoiling from the tangle of air hose and fishing nets to go snaking over the side, when I suddenly realized it was not attached to anything. I yelled to Harry, who was sitting in the stern, and, like a flash, his left hand shot out and grabbed the rope as it whipped by, thus saving them the expense of a new anchor.

A couple of years later we acquired a small boat of our own. It was a double-hulled, fourteen feet long, fibreglass trifoil, painted a lovely sunshine yellow. We bought her from a colleague at Akrotiri, who was posted back to the UK, and re-christened her THE HAWK. With a 45 HP Johnson outboard motor, the journey to Kingfisher Bay took very little time. Our family, and friends who sometimes came with us, never failed to be overwhelmed by the beauty of the place. To swim in those clear, warm waters was an experience never to be forgotten.

Yiangos, one of Latchi's most colourful characters.
Yiangos.

One summer, our friends from Droushia decided they would take lessons in diving, so, after much careful planning and organization, they set off from Latchi with their Dutch diving instructor, Walter, for their first foray into the deep. As they were absolute beginners, Walter had decided that a good place to introduce them to the underwater world would be Kingfisher Bay. When they arrived it was deserted, save for a couple with their five-year-old son who, having hired a boat for the morning, were enjoying a picnic on the beach.

The divers began to attire themselves for the forthcoming ordeal. The head of the family, who is six feet seven inches tall and hefty with it, was crammed into an XL size wet suit and, with aqualung strapped on and mask and mouthpiece in place, he was soon in the shallow water learning the rudiments of diving. He learned how to give and recognize the thumbs up signal, which means 'going up' and the thumb and forefinger circled signal, meaning 'everything is OK'. Rapidly gaining in confidence, he decided it was time to try a deep dive. He moved into deeper water near the small island and, going down, was lost in delight at the wonderful underwater vista opening up before his very eyes. He was feeling more than pleased with himself for having progressed to a real dive on the first lesson when, suddenly, the five-year-old child swam down past him, wearing a little plastic snorkel mask and tube.

Kingfisher Bay is no longer the hidden paradise it was in those early days, but it is still as beautiful and the kingfishers still nest there, and, for the price of the ride, Yiangos, one of Latchi's most colourful characters, will take you there in his lovely old fishing boat the KOUL-LA, where you will enjoy traditional *souvla*, a glass of wine or two and a swim in those magical, turquoise waters.

[NOTE: The story of Alkione was told to me by the local people although I believe that in Greek Mythology, Alcyone, wife of Ceyx, threw herself into the sea after her husband was drowned. The Gods changed them both into kingfishers and the sea is said to be calm when they are nesting.]

It was inevitable that tourist development would, sooner or later, encroach on Latchi. With the beautiful coastline in the north of Cyprus occupied by the Turks, and the magnificent area of Ayia Napa very overdeveloped, the eyes of the package tour operators, and others seeking to become millionaires, turned to this coast. Local Cypriots, who, in earlier years, had to emigrate to find work, were now coming home to find that their family land was in a prime area for tourism. Who can blame them for wanting to return to their homeland and, at the same time, make a fortune, or at least a comfortable living, from their heritage? Unfortunately, change sometimes brings its negative aspects to the nature lover, and it is sad to see large tracts of land bulldozed into sterile plateaux, where once stood lovely slopes of pine trees beneath which bloomed cistus and wild orchids, including that king of rare orchids here, the striking yellow Orchis Punctulata. Some of the ancient tombs, where in past years, shepherds found Byzantine jewellery of gold filigree set with turquoises, have been filled in to make room for yet another restaurant or apartments, and holiday villas for wealthy Europeans to spend a few weeks a year in, looking like ice-cream factories with their gaudy paintwork of yellow, blue, pink and green, stand where once Barlia Robertiana bloomed in profusion. These orchids are officially protected, but you can always tell when a local flower lover has been by when they are in bloom. The leaves will be scattered along the road where they have been uprooted to be planted in the garden next to the daisies and geraniums. Of course, they never survive to come up again the following year, but, never mind, there are plenty more to dig up.

A botanist, who takes parties of orchid enthusiasts on trips overseas, sometimes calls me when she is in Cyprus to see which orchids are in bloom in our area. One year she arrived in the village with a coachload of eager passengers who were bristling with expensive camera equipment. As they disembarked from the bus, one keen member of the party spotted a Barlia, or giant orchid in full flower in a garden. The others gathered round and a hush fell as they gazed reverently at this rare sight. The door opened and the lady of the house, a warm-hearted and extremely hospitable woman, seeing that these foreigners were enchanted with the flower, obligingly bent down, picked it and offered it to them.

When we first came here everyone thought we were mad. "It's so far away" they said "there's nothing to do there". Similar comments were passed by Cypriot and English friends alike. Now, everyone wants to be here, we are suddenly fashionable as the last unspoilt bastion of the island. Latchi, with its plethora of excellent fish restaurants, becomes very crowded in July and August, and, when the factories in the big towns close for the annual holiday, the beaches and surrounding fields fill up with campers. It becomes a lengthy chore to drive to nearby Polis Chrysochous to go to the bank or the post office. I love meeting people but, on our beach, I infinitely prefer turtles to tourists, so we decided to withdraw a bit inside our own territory. We had a big space, with poor soil and underlying rock, between the house and the studio, so we determined to sell our boat and build a swimming pool. As usual, we didn't have much money so could not elect to build one outright, and, in any case, we couldn't face the thought of having to go through 'no problems' again. The obvious solution was to build it ourselves. We might have had second thoughts if we had known what we were letting ourselves in for, but, at the time, it seemed like a good idea.

First we laid it out with much measuring and sighting and tripping over balls of string, as Harry made sure everything was parallel to everything else. Every time we swam in the sea we tried all kinds of experiments to see how deep we needed it and how much area would give us a good swim. Once we were satisfied, we contacted the best JCB operator in the area and asked him to come and start excavating.

Sotiris and his digger are famous in Polis, where he lives. Good looking and self-assured, he is extremely skilful, but not known for his forbearance, and the morning he was due to arrive, we heard a roaring and clanking as he came up the dirt track like a racing driver at Brands Hatch. We had taken the precaution of removing the front gate and part of the fence, which was just as well, because a little thing like that would not have stopped Sotiris once he'd got his working area in his sights. Off he went and very soon earth began piling up and up and..... We stopped to drink coffee and he saw me glancing apprehensively at the huge pile of earth accumulating behind him. He assured us there was no problem ("oh no", we groaned inwardly). There was no point in paying unnecessarily for lorries to come and take it away, he would get rid of it as he went along, and, sure enough, he did. When it looked as though he would never be able to get his machine out of the garden again, he swung round, and, locking the bucket, bulldozed the mound down, repeatedly driving over it and pushing it ahead of him. As the excavation progressed, we had masses of spare soil, but he disposed of it all by sprinkling it up and down the roadway outside (well, it WAS a dirt track anyway), covering over some unsightly rubble that someone else had dumped at the top of our lane, raising the level of the area where we grow our fruit trees and altering the rate of incline of our driveway, not to mention completely burying the lower garden terrace. We were relieved to find that the strata of very hard rock, running underneath the house, only went across a small corner of the pool and the expensive-to-hire *pistola,* needed to break it up, was already coming to the village for something else, so the work was completed in a couple of days.

We now had a massive hole in the ground, much bigger than the nine by five metres the pool would eventually become, and we needed a lot of reinforcing steel before any thought of concreting could arise. These steel rods come in lengths of twelve metres and are somewhat difficult to move about. We solved this problem with the help of a friend of ours who had a building project going on in the nearby village of Prodhromi. Hitching our boat trailer up to the jeep, we went to his site where we used his machine to cut the steels into suitable lengths, load them on the trailer and drive, rattling and bumping, back here again. People in Latchi came to their doors to see what was going on as we made dozens of trips to and fro. Then came the hard slog for Harry, who had to fix all the rods in position. He planned to build the walls of the pool with big concrete blocks, reinforced with steel rods and infilled with concrete. Before the walls could be built, however, the base of the pool had to be floated in all in one go, and this called for the services of the *pompa.*

Another team of experts arrived, driving a huge machine with long, swivelling, hydraulic pipes and coils of flexible hose through which concrete could be poured into our swimming pool. There was one slight drawback. Following the excavation, the driveway was now too steep for the contraption to get anywhere near the pool and it had to stay down near where the front gate used to be. Nothing daunts the Cypriot workman though - he thrives on challenges of a technical nature. He is a master at the art of the botch-up. Faced with the impossible, his sheer inventiveness boggles the mind. From any old stuff lying around he will contrive a botch of impressive magnitude and, what is more, it will work. I am convinced that Heath Robinson was a Cypriot. Our team, with the inevitable "no problem", ferreted around behind the garden shed and came up with several sheets of corrugated tin with which they constructed chutes, of varying sizes, leading from the pool towards their hose. At the same time they added more hose until they estimated the two would meet. This was somewhere over a couple of beautiful hibiscus bushes. These preliminaries over, they began mixing their concrete in a huge mobile mixer which was parked in the road outside, next to the piles of sand and gravel and bags of cement that Harry had provided.

While this was going on, Harry was down in the pit putting the last minute touches to his work and carefully placing boards to stand on, so that no one would tread on the steels and bend them out of alignment.

"Take very good care" he said to me "to see that they start at this end and pour slowly, so that I can level it with my plank. Concrete must always be poured slowly anyway".

Well, these were the proverbial famous last words if ever I heard any. The *pompa* started up and, suddenly, torrents of very liquid concrete gushed out of the hose, splashed somewhere near the chute, and, eventually, started hurtling into the pool. Within minutes, Harry was up to the knees in wet concrete, all thought of trying not to tread on the steels forgotten, as he, and one of the team of experts, frantically threw out all the planks before they became totally submerged. Thankfully, he managed to retrieve his wellies, which had been washed away in the avalanche, but anything else we overlooked must still be down there some-where.

The following weeks were arduous ones for Harry, but, gradually, the walls were completed and tons of concrete was poured outside them, with the help of a succession of friends who turned up on various occasions. We were then ready to plaster the inside of the pool.

When we were in the process of building the house, we did a lot of the internal plastering ourselves, because, at the time, we were unable to find anyone to do it. As the procedure was quite different from the familiar English method, I was sent down to a nearby building site to 'spy' - my instructions being to find out the correct mix and how to apply it. I returned with the secret formula scribbled on a piece of paper and the news that they flung it on the walls from a flat trowel, using a flick of the wrist, rather like making a drop shot in tennis.
"OK" said Harry, "you're the tennis player, I'll mix it, you fling it", and this we did, getting a lot more skilful at it as we went along. Now the experience paid dividends and we made an excellent job of plastering the inside of the pool. Landscaping was falling into place around it and, every time I went into Paphos, I brought back a load of flagstones for the surrounds. At last, it was beginning to look like a proper swimming pool. Then came the day we were ready to paint it with the special paint.

This paint came with all kinds of instructions, the most important being that there should only be twenty-four hours between the application of coats and the surfaces must be absolutely dry and dust-free each time. Moreover, not one single fly must set foot or wing on the area we were painting, as, once stuck in the harden-er, it would become like a sharp needle when it dried. We were so keen not to make a hash of it that we even rang the Meteorological Office at Akrotiri and ascertained that the weather would be good. The base coat, complete with hardener, went on and we were surprised to find how much quicker and easier it was than we had anticipated. In high spirits, we woke the next morning and checked again with the Meteorological Office. This time, the painting was more of a task, but, with Harry doing all the difficult bits with a brush, and me tackling all the easy bits with a roller, our pool soon took on its beautiful blue colour. We gazed at it in admiration and congratulated ourselves. A bit too soon, as it happened, for, within half an hour, someone below us at Latchi had cut a field of corn and a million small black flies swarmed our way. Soon the appearance of the pool was virtually all black. We could not believe this. One fly was supposed to be a disaster - if these all turned needle sharp, the only people who would be able to swim in our pool would be Indian Yogis. In despair, we telephoned the manufacturer of the paint and he said that, notwithstanding there must only be twenty-four hours between the application of each coat, we would have to get this all off and ensure the surfaces were clean, dry and dust-free before we started again.

The following day Harry got busy with the sander, and, another of my bright ideas having occurred to me, I rushed over the mountain into Paphos where I purchased several metres of net curtaining. I freely admit I am not much good with a needle, in fact, Harry knows only too well if he gets a hole in his sock he might as well throw it away, but this situation called for desperate measures. Once home, it took me altogether seven hours to hack together a huge net which would cover the entire pool, and could be held down by planks around the edge, while we worked in dust and fly-free bliss beneath.

Harry had finished sanding down the walls, brushed up the dust, washed them again and now they were drying nicely. We went to bed, exhausted, only to wake up in the night to hear thunder rumbling and, shortly afterwards, torrential rain coming down. In the morning, not only was there a lot of water lying round in the pool, but half the Sahara desert too, for this was the annual sand-laden rain from Africa, which, when it dries out, leaves a reddish-brown deposit all over your windows, clean washing and, in this case, our pool. Back to square one and we cleaned and dried it again and waited another day and another..... Eventually we got the go-ahead from the weather men at Akrotiri, crawled into the sweat-tank under the net, and completed the job.

Was it all worth it? As I sit here by the finished pool, set in its natural rock amphitheatre amid the green pines and carobs, with clouds of rose-pink oleander and sky-blue plumbago in full bloom around me, windowboxes and earthenware pots are spilling their petunias and geraniums in a riot of colour and a beautiful swallowtail butterfly sways drunkenly in the scent of newly-watered lavender. A huge red dragonfly is hovering - admiring its reflection in the crystal depths, while, statue-like, one of our big rock lizards is gazing at it longingly. Swallows are sweeping low over the water and the little pied wheatear is fluffed contentedly over her eggs in the nest box attached to the studio wall. Soon, when the sun's rays intensify, I will slide into the cool water and later, if the humidity is high and sleep eludes us, we will step from the bedroom door, into a night scented with jasmine and lemon flowers, and swim together in the moon-washed pool. Was it all worth it? Without a doubt.

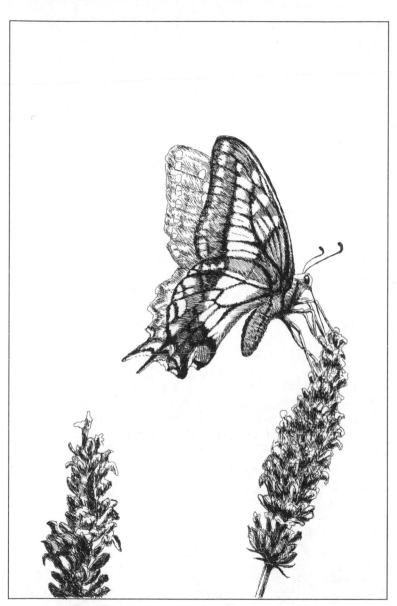

A beautiful swallowtail butterfly.
Swallowtail Butterfly.

CHAPTER 9

SPRINGTIME IN CYPRUS

Springtime in Cyprus is truly a sight to behold. After the winter rains, the dry, buff-coloured landscape, burnt by the fierce heat of summer, turns green as fields of wheat, corn and barley wave in the breeze and new green leaves appear on the grape vines. Fields of scarlet poppies and yellow rape appear and, in Akamas, wild cyclamen flower profusely. Here, in secluded areas, there are drifts of a rare, dark red tulip which grows only in this region of Cyprus. Red, too, are the anemones, said to have sprung up where droplets of blood from the slain Adonis fell to earth, when the beautiful youth, much loved by Aphrodite, was killed by a wild boar. Other anemones, from all shades of deep purple down through violet and pink to white, cover the ground and wild orchids bloom in profusion. The hedgerows in Paphos abound with bright yellow mimosa, dripping its blossom at the roadside, and, in the scrub, pink, white and yellow rock roses, together with delicate cream and yellow ranunculas, flower alongside the golden broom. Whole fields are coloured a deep pink with wild gladioli, called *Loulouthia tou Pasqua* by the local people. The almond trees are in blossom, looking like hundreds of powder-puffs in the valleys, and over all is the heady scent of orange blossom from the citrus groves, where the trees are decked out in their spring flowers like so many brides.

It will soon be the Greek Orthodox Easter, the biggest event of the year, and there is much preparation in the village, as all the plastered walls get a fresh coat of whitewash and the big bread ovens are stacked with

The big bread ovens are stacked with brushwood.
Bread Oven.

brushwood. On Good Friday the young, unmarried girls spread out into the surrounding fields gathering spring flowers to decorate the bier, which, that night, will carry the icon of Christ crucified - the only night of the year that it will be uncovered. In the afternoon they go into the church to sing special songs, while the canopied, wooden bier is gradually bedecked with flowers. During the service it will be paraded around the outside of the church and the bearers will stand in the doorway, the holy icon held high, while all the villagers pass underneath. Everyone goes to church at Easter, most of them attending all the long religious celebrations. We go too, but never manage to stay the whole course of the service which, for us, is very difficult to understand.

One Easter Sunday, our close friend and neighbour, Alfons, decided to go to church to show willing. Alfons, a former officer with the Austrian contingent of the United Nations in Cyprus, is a great wit with a marvellous sense of humour. He and his wife, Helli, live in their house here for most of the year, returning to their home in Austria for about three months in the winter. He went up to the church that Easter Sunday morning, thinking he would slip quietly in at the back and catch the last twenty minutes or so of the special service. When he got there the church was empty, and, assuming he was too late, he went to sit in the coffee shop for a while. There, a forestry officer, who speaks reasonable English, assured him that there was a bit of a delay but proceedings at the church would definitely start at twelve noon. Alfons sat quietly drinking his coffee and then ordering another, so that he wouldn't be one of the first to arrive and feel conspicuous. At about a quarter past twelve, he returned to the, now crowded, church where he lit a candle, put it in a holder and crept to the back to secrete himself behind one of the big wooden pews. This was a mistake. In Cyprus, this area is reserved strictly for women, the men (of course) being allocated all the pews at the front. Suddenly, he noticed the forestry officer and the priest apparently signalling to him to come forward. Looking over his shoulder to be sure there was no one else there, he realized, with increasing dread, that they were indeed addressing him. Now in the limelight, which he had desperately been trying to avoid, he sidled up to them only to have a large book thrust into his hands.

"Quick" hissed the forestry man, "part of this special service for Easter has to be sung in German, and you are the only one who can do it".

Not believing what he was hearing, Alfons studied the text and, sure enough, it was written in Greek, English and German. He was getting the part of Doubting Thomas in German. The priest would sing the same part in Greek and one of our former neighbours, Elias, had been commandeered to sing the English part. Likeable Elias, while an extremely competent electrician, speaks English about as well as I speak Swahili, and Alfons can't sing in tune, but, with admirable determination in the face of impending disaster, he staunchly clutched the microphone and somehow managed to shout his contribution at the appropriate time. Everyone appeared satisfied and there were murmurs of approval all round, but the resulting three-part harmony would not exactly have made an entry for the Eisteddfod. Ever since this event, Alfons has been trying all kinds of other ways to show willing.

Once *Christos Anesti* has been repeated over and over and the proper reply given, the Easter celebrations can begin in earnest. Sunday is a family day with much feasting and merrymaking over family get-togethers. The traditional red, hardboiled eggs are knocked together, the idea being to crack your opponent's egg instead of your own (rather like the English game of conkers). This is the time for *flaounes* - peculiar only to

Cyprus, no Easter would be complete without the tantalizing smell of these pastry squares which are folded over on to a filling of local cheese, eggs and sultanas.

A bar is set up in the square near the church and a lorryload of red plastic chairs brought in. *Bouzouki* players accompany singing and traditional Greek dancing, and on Easter Monday there is a donkey race up through the main street of the village, the contestants taking part painstakingly decorating their mounts with flowers and rosettes and, sometimes, the occasional L plate. Various competitions follow, the noisiest and most popular event the Tug O' War, when our village team competes with the strongmen from all the surrounding villages. We always do well in this one, our anchor man, Nicos, being built like a Japanese Sumo wrestler.

By Easter, the weather is beginning to warm up and the spring migration is under way. Large numbers of birds arrive to spend the summer and we look forward to seeing many familiar ones taking up residence in and around the garden again. It is also an interesting challenge to try and identify the many migrant birds passing through. One bright, sunny morning in April, I was up in the kitchen making some tea. There was an exceptionally strong wind blowing and, without warning, a strangely-marked bird dropped on to the kitchen window-sill and stayed there without moving, obviously totally exhausted. I was able to examine it at close quarters and, once I had consulted the well-thumbed bird book, realized that it was a wryneck woodpecker. After a couple of hours it had recovered enough to fly down into the garden, where I lost sight of it and did not see it again that year. Every subsequent year though, just one has appeared in the garden on its spring migration. It usually stays in under the hedge feeding all day before moving on. This spring, I stood for a long time on the verandah watching as it gorged itself on ants from a big nest it had found, its head bobbing up and down rhythmically like one of those perpetual motion toys. The following day it had gone. I am sorry they don't stay near us to breed, for I would very much like to offer this attractive bird the hospitality of one of our nest boxes.

Many colourful birds begin to appear at this time. The golden oriole arrives each spring with a loud, flutey, whistle. He is a big, strikingly-coloured bird with a bright yellow body and black wings, and he comes to the birdbath for a long drink before secreting himself in various trees in the garden. Surprisingly, despite his brilliant colour, he is not easy to find as he moves silently from branch to branch, well-disguised by the yellow of carob leaves that are ready to drop and the black of any unharvested carobs from last year.

Another bright yellow and black bird flies in at this time and his behaviour always follows the same pattern. The smaller black-headed bunting, with his canary yellow body and all-black head, is quickly spotted because of his habit of always singing from the topmost branches of the trees and not varying his sweetly tuneful, but repetitive, song.

For sheer magic of colour though, first prize has to go to the bee-eaters. Always feeding in flocks, a musical warbling heralds their arrival down the valley to our garden, where they swoop and soar and glide, landing in the trees around us or on the electricity wires to consume their prey. We planted a hedge of rosemary around the lower orchard and it is always alive and buzzing with wild bees in the summer months. Each time a bee-eater catches one in its long beak, it flies up to whack its victim, on a wire or branch, before throwing back its head and swallowing it, like a seabird swallowing a fish. Their beauty is breathtaking as they sweep overhead, the sun highlighting their multi-coloured plumage of turquoise, green, yellow, chestnut and black.

Here, in this bright sunshine and clear light, colours glow vibrantly and none more so than those provided by nature. One sun-baked, lizard-lazy day I was looking down the valley, where the shimmering heat haze made the fronds of dried grasses move in the windless air and the sea diffuse into the amethyst mountains behind, when there was a flash of colour and a roller flew past, executing a perfect barrel roll, the glorious blue of its plumage standing out against the dark green of the carob and cypress trees. The Scops owls had hatched a few days earlier and they purred and scrabbled in their box, from time to time, as they woke from their daytime dozing. I could hear the female francolin calling to her brood and, knowing they would be glad of a drink and some cool, damp earth on a day like this, I went down into the garden to switch on the electric pump that brings water up out of the well for the trees. I stood in the shade of the lemon tree, enjoying the tangy scents, for this variety bears blossom, green and ripe fruit all at the same time, giving us a constant supply of fresh lemons. With the water flowing, numerous small birds came to flit in and out of the branches and, suddenly, I found myself standing in a cloud of butterflies. They were all around me like snowflakes - bright yellow, orange, white, lavender blue and the incredibly beautiful swallowtails. I stood there hardly daring to breathe, lest the magic of the moment be lost.

The greenfinches had brought their fledglings to the birdbath to drink, and, as the level of the water had dropped with the baths already taken that morning, I turned on the garden tap to refill it. As I moved to pick up the end of the hosepipe, two pairs of red-rumped swallows began to wheel and circle around me. They landed, one at a time, on the wet stones beneath the pedestal, then took off again to continue circling. I filled the wells around some of the shrubs with water, and, instantly, they all landed and began paddling around and picking up mud, taking no notice of me standing

One sun-baked, lizard-lazy day.
Lazy Lizard.

there. They began to cruise around the house, flying in under the arches and verandahs, sometimes actually clinging to the wall, but they did not build. They flew off, instead, in the direction of the rock tombs across the road, but I live in hope that they will eventually build under the shelter of our verandahs and become another lot of permanent house guests.

After the owls, the second lot of lodgers to move in with us were small black and white, truly Cypriot, birds. It was not long after the studio had been finished when I saw a pair of Cyprus pied wheatears flying all around it, landing on window ledges and shutters, even flying right inside and out again. I guessed they were looking for a suitable nest site so, once again, I approached my long-suffering spouse and asked him to make a nest box.

"You design it and I'll make it" he said.

I had seen these little birds nesting up in under over-hanging stones in the lane, so we made a simple box with a small upright bar of wood across the front, to stop the fledglings falling out, and a long, sloping roof to overhang the whole thing. This we attached to the studio wall, and, within minutes, the female had inspected it and they were flying round the garden collecting nesting material. There is an old copper coffee jug on a low wall underneath, and to the front of, the nest box and the female always lands on there before flying up into the box. The male bird never bothers, he simply flies straight in and out again. As soon as the wheatears begin to arrive at the end of March, I know it will not be long before ours are in residence. The box stays from year to year, but the female always adds to it before she lays her eggs. I know she is almost ready when I find her at the front doormat, pilfering the coarse hairs to weave into her nest. They raise two broods every year and are attractive and interesting little characters. If a cat or a snake appears in the vicinity when they have

The female always lands on there.
Cyprus Pied Wheatear.

fledglings, they will hover over the intruder, fly straight at it or try to lead it away, all the time making a great deal of noise. If we are in the garden, they will fly agitatedly between us and the source of danger to alert us. An ornithologist told me that they overwinter in the Sudan, but breed only in Cyprus, and nowhere else in the world. Once or twice we have had a bit of a tragedy and found their lovely blue, red-spotted eggs smashed on the floor, where a big lizard has managed to get at them, and, a couple of times the fledglings have left the nest, just when the sand-laden rain storms hit us for a few days during May, and have perished in the cold. Nevertheless, they usually manage to raise two or three out of the two sets of fledglings and have become a permanent part of our household.

Fascinating as all these birds are, none can stir the emotions as much as those which appear for only three weeks or so in April, as they rest before continuing their journey up into the mountain areas to breed. These are the nightingales, and our garden is filled with them at times. In the early mornings we lie awake listening to their magical song. No wonder these birds are legendary, for, to hear a nightingale sing, is to undergo one of life's most poignant experiences. Sometimes I see them feeding on the ground or coming to drink at one of the birdbaths. Fairly big, brown birds, with lovely eyes and a reddish tail, they spend most of the time hidden in the hedge or thicket and they sing during daylight hours. Once, when I was in the garden, I sat, unmoving, for almost an hour while, a few feet away in the shrubbery, a nightingale sang without stopping, hardly repeating the same phrase, the pure, liquid notes tumbling like drops of crystal in the clear air. It wasn't until it had stopped that I realized there were tears running down my face.

Since the completion of the swimming pool the number of swallows in the area has increased. They beautify the electricity wires I had thought so ugly when they were first installed, and, from the upstairs windows, I watch lines of fledglings perched, like rows of clothes pegs, preening their feathers and flipping their wings to be fed every time an adult bird approaches. With their faster flight they take water directly from the swimming pool. They don't mind at all if someone is in there swimming at the time, they simply swoop down, grab a beakful, and soar up again, their white underparts turned a lovely blue by the reflection of the water. Our grandchildren are delighted when they are here and a dozen or more swallows dive-bomb them as they are practising their lengths. The children love to sit on the still-warm flagstones after dusk, with the floodlight illuminating the pool, and watch tiny bats swooping silently around, sometimes dipping to drink and sending out concentric ripples across the water.

One night, not long ago, we were fast asleep in bed when I woke to feel something brushing past my hair. I was instantly wide awake, alerted to thoughts of all kinds of unpleasant visitations, but a look all round the head of the bed with a torch revealed nothing, so we settled down again. We then heard a sound like a ceiling fan rotating, and, again, something brushed past my hair. This time Harry got out of bed and switched on the light and there, zooming round the room, was a small bat. We could not open the window for it to go out as they are protected with mosquito screens in the bedrooms, so Harry opened the front door. Our intruder did not take the hint, so I suggested we might turn off the bedroom light and switch on the one outside in the porch.

"I don't know what you're making such a fuss about" said Harry, standing, unclad, in the bathroom doorway " it's only a harmless little bat", and, so saying, he mistakenly switched on the light in the bathroom instead of the one in the porch. At this point, Dracula's cousin made a frantic dash straight towards the source of the light, causing the naked hero to shriek in alarm, and, in trying to duck and avoid the harmless little bat, he banged his head and shut his finger in the door.

A large body of water, like a swimming pool, is bound to be an attraction to all kinds of creatures, particularly in the hot, dry climate of summer, and ours produces the odd surprise now and then. One night Old Nick appeared. If ever a name suited a particular creature, this one does, for Old Nick is a hedgehog, but unlike any I have ever seen before. Hedgehogs, exactly like those in England, are quite common in Cyprus, in fact, there are usually several to be found squashed on the roads in the mornings, victims of cars unmindful of their preoccupied noctambulation. They can be heard after dark snuffling around in the garden under the carob trees, and, one morning, we were dismayed to find an enormous one drowned in the pool. Most things that fall in during the night, manage to rest on the flaps of the skimmer boxes and keep their heads above water until we arrive to fish them out with a net. We regularly have tiny green tree frogs, beautifully camouflaged toads, small lizards and shrews (who are excellent swimmers, even swimming well underwater), but the unfortunate hedgehog was too heavy and the flap simply went down under his weight, causing him to sink. They say the devil looks after his own, so perhaps that's why Old Nick wasn't the victim. He is like a caricature of a hedgehog. Much thinner than an ordinary one and with longer legs, on which he moves with great alacrity if we happen to disturb him on one of his nightly excursions in the garden. He has very long ears, which seem far too big for his body, and an elongated snout, which turns up at the end, giving him an evil and sinister appearance - hence the name. I haven't mentioned him to anyone in the village. I'm not sure what the local people would make of Old Nick, in a place where even something as charming as a small owl is dubbed a 'devil bird'.

CHAPTER 10

ARACHNOPHOBIA

Arachne was a skilful weaver who challenged Athene to a contest. Athene tore the work up and, when Arachne hanged herself, she changed her into a spider.

The warmer weather sometimes brings less welcome visitors to our house. One night, having dined on swordfish steaks at Latchi, we returned home after dark and switched on the light in the hall to see the biggest spider in the world half-way up the stairs. It was black and hairy and, as we were soon to discover, could move at something approaching the speed of light. Taking a sweeping brush, Harry attempted to persuade this monster to come down the stairs and out of the front door. Instead, it accelerated down the stairs and into our bedroom. I immediately began to consider the possibilities of getting someone to take us in for the night, because there was no way I was going to sleep in the bedroom, or even the house, with that THING in there. Harry said "Don't panic, I'll find it and kill it".

A thorough search ensued, taking ages and revealing nothing, until we heard a rattling, metallic sound over near the window. He pulled back the curtain and there IT was, scuttling across the wire mesh mosquito grille which was blocking its exit from the window. With admirable quick thinking, Harry slid the window shut, neatly trapping it in the intervening space. Good thinking, now how do we dispose of it? I then had a bright idea. We still had some spray, provided by the RAF for use in married quarters, which is supposed to deal with all flies and mosquitos, creepy-crawlies and other nasties in general. Gingerly opening the window a fraction, we gave it a long burst and hurriedly shut the window again. Understandably, it did not like this very much and streaked frantically around the protective screen like a demented catherine wheel. We did not want it to suffer a lingering death, so repeated bursts followed until it was soaking wet and still tearing around in its confined space. We left the window shut and retired upstairs for a cup of coffee. When we returned it was, more or less, motionless and Harry bravely scooped it into a plastic container. I wanted to preserve it in some spirit (actually, we use the local moonshine firewater called *zivania*) but was unable to find any, so, with razor sharp thinking, I put it into the freezer for the time being. I was anxious to know more about these things. Were they poisonous? Did they bite? and so on. I knew just the person to ask.

Snake George arrived on his motor bike and examined the spider, which was now floating in a specimen jar.

"Ah yes" he breathed "zis is ze African bird-eating spider".

"It eats BIRDS?" said Harry, disbelievingly.

(I believed it all right, from the look of this thing, it could easily have polished off an ostrich for breakfast and looked round for more). George explained that, here in Cyprus, these nocturnal carnivores live mainly on small lizards, baby mice and large flies and insects. The thought of the web one of these things might weave was enough to give even the stout-hearted night-mares, but George assured us that they do not make webs, in fact this is why they move so fast; they have to dash out and grab their prey, immobilizing it with a swift injection from their fangs.

None of this comforted me very much. I had faced up to rats, mice, cockroaches, scorpions and snakes, but this thing gave me the horrors. George told us that our garden, with so many rocks and flowers attracting all kinds of things they like to eat, was an ideal habitat for them. They live in underground holes which have more than one exit. Pointing to an upturned metal drum, on which some planks were resting, he indicated that this would be a likely hideout. It was near the garden tap and under a carob tree where the fallen leaves create a humus, providing the hot, moist atmosphere they like to live in. He approached the drum and, removing the planks, pulled it aside. Sure enough there were two circular holes drilled into the baked earth beneath. He let a trickle of water from the hosepipe go down one hole and said they would now leave, and, providing we removed the drum from the vicinity, would go away and find someone else to haunt. He turned the drum upright and gave a triumphant cry. There, on the inside of the drum, were two more of the ghastly creatures, although these were not as big as our original model. Asking for a small plastic bowl, he deftly captured them both and put them in the specimen boxes he always carried with him. A few metres away we noticed a bird tackling something quite big and, on investigation, it turned out to be yet another of these spiders, this one lifeless and with one leg missing. He decided he would keep it in spirit and, before putting it in one of his containers, said he would show us why it was prudent not to let them stay in the house, where they have a penchant for concealing themselves in the wardrobe. Taking a pair of forceps from his pocket, he withdrew from the spider a wicked-looking pair of fangs, like two slightly-curved needles, which retracted again as soon as he released them. He said the bite is not fatal, but the puncture wounds made by the fangs can easily become infected and cause a lot of trouble, and the pain is considerable.

"Don't kill them" he urged, "just catch them and put them outside in the garden".

Well, I have never confessed this to Snake George but, on the few occasions when we have had these awful spiders in the house, we (well, actually, Harry) always deal with them in the ingenious manner we devised once when we found one on the ceiling. Terrified it would drop off on to us, we got the mop for swabbing floors, wet it and squeezed it almost dry; then Harry carefully stalked the enemy knowing that, if he startled it, it would take off at a phenomenal speed. Once he managed to get the mop positioned right underneath, he gave a sudden upward thrust and trapped it. Due to the fact that their bodies, although big and hairy, are rather soft, over the years we have accumulated a few black splodges on our ceiling where we have mopped them to death.

There was a sequel to Snake George's visit. About a week later he telephoned me to say "Sheila, you vill not belief it". He said that, when he returned home after ridding us of our barrel of spiders, he was, as usual, very late, so he released the two he had captured from the drum into his garden and put the container, with the dead one inside, on the bench in his garage, intending to deal with it later. Five days later, he suddenly remembered he had left it there and, knowing his wife would be furious if she came across it, thought he had better dispose of it. He opened the container and the 'dead' spider leapt out and ran up his arm into his hair (which, fortunately for him, is very thick). He instinctively brushed it off and saw it drop on to the ground where, even with one leg missing, it scuttled at great speed into the garden and disappeared.

When I think about how persevering these things are, I don't feel so bad about the mop.

Of course, there are others psychologically better equipped to deal with these arachnids than I. Take my son, for instance. One spring he came from England to

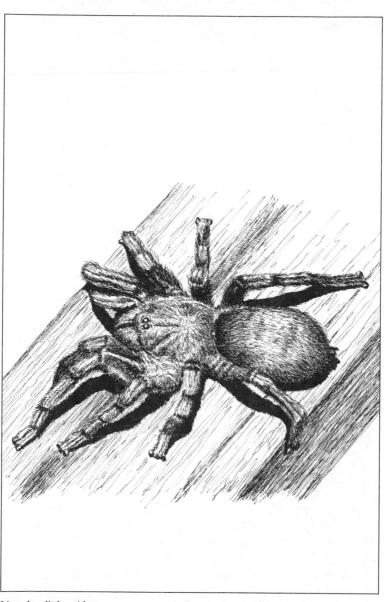

It's only a little spider.
African Bird-eating Spider.

stay for a few weeks. He is well acquainted with the island and its people and shares my interest in all things natural. One night I had gone down to bed first and was just opening a book to read when I happened to glance up and there, on the wall just below the ceiling, was one of the dreaded black monsters, and this one was MASSIVE. Carl Lewis couldn't have beaten me to the door and I called for help as I went.

Slowly down the stairs came the intrepid duo, father and son, with extremely patronizing remarks like "Don't make such a fuss", "It's only a little spider", "Anyway, they're not that big", "We won't kill it, will we Dad? We'll put the poor little thing outside", and more of this ilk until they reached the bedroom door, when a stunned silence ensued.

"Now that is a BIG spider. OK, Dad, show me how you deal with them".

"Well, it's probably better if you do it, you never know when you may be in on your own".

"OK, er, well - if you open the patio door I'll just, er, guide it towards you".

"Right".

"OK, er, I didn't realize they were as big as this - I'll just stand on here and aaarrrgghh..."

"Aaarrrgghh..."

"They really move fast don't they?"

"Yes, well mind it doesn't drop off on you".

"OK. Now, er, I'd better not touch it with my hand, these things bite don't they?"

"Yes, they don't kill you though, it's just very painful".

"Ah, er, well, in that case I'll just find something to..."

While this riveting conversation was going on I was beginning to get decidedly chilly, standing outside in the garden, and very much wanted to go back to bed, besides which, I thought the spider might outwit them, while they were making up their minds, and secrete itself somewhere else in the bedroom. This was no time to be messing about looking for 'something to move it with'.

"I've got the very thing" I said, from the safety of the open front doorway, and handed them the mop.

Both our children love Cyprus, having been to school here during our tours of duty with the Royal Air Force, and they come out whenever time and finances permit. One spring, we were getting the house ready for a visit from our daughter with her husband and three small children. Rozi, the youngest, was only a few months old and I borrowed a cot, push chair and high chair and gave the place an extra clean. I bought Milton to sterilize the bottles and, in general, tried to ensure that the place was hygienic and ready to receive a new baby.

This was when the rat appeared. We first kept seeing signs where it had been on the upstairs front verandah then, one evening, when we were sitting outside enjoying the moonlight, it poked its head down through the trellis and looked at us. It was actually quite a pretty creature, not one of the big, brown carob rats, but a rather dainty, silver-grey, field rat with long whiskers and inquisitive eyes. We felt very bad but, there was no question about it, with a small baby coming, the rat would have to go.

I went into Polis and acquired a rat-trap, like an old-fashioned mouse-trap, which is baited with a piece of cheese and, when the unsuspecting rodent grabs it, a metal bar whips over and breaks its neck.

"It's mercifully quick" said Harry, "it won't feel a thing". He was right, it didn't. We heard the WHAP of the trap shutting later that night and slid back the window to find the cheese gone and the trap empty.

"I'll set it so it will spring at the touch of a whisker" said Harry.

Two days later the score was Rat nine, Harry nil.

I went into the Agricultural Office and consulted the experts. "No problem" they said. I winced, but accepted the small squares, which looked like pieces of pink chewing-gum, and which, they assured me, would finish him off in no time. What is more, he would push off and die somewhere else and not make a nasty smell on my verandah. I thanked them and hurried home with this prodigious stuff and, telling Harry that he'd got entirely the wrong idea and the task called for a more modern, scientific approach, I placed a few pieces on a tin lid in the war zone. Two hours later they had all gone.

"The poor little devil has gone away to die" I said sadly. Later that evening, having finished dinner, we took our coffee out on to the verandah, only to find the rat had beaten us to it and was poking its head down through the trellis and looking very healthy indeed. After that, obviously having taken a liking to the stuff, it wolfed down every piece I put out and came back for more.

I returned to the Agricultural Office.

"Ah" they said, "you have a resistant rat. You must nail this thing near where you have seen it run".

'This thing' was an evil-looking square of a blue substance resembling candlewax, and I was duly warned that it was VERY poisonous - I should even wear gloves when handling it. Returning home, I nailed it up above the trellis and withdrew. We did not see the enemy again that night but, on inspection in the morning, found teeth marks on the square. We looked knowingly at each other, the deed was done.

Below the verandah is another patio, outside the spare bedroom, and here we keep a small refrigerator stocked with cold drinks for visiting guests. The next morning I was watering the bougainvillea when I suddenly saw the rat go in underneath this fridge. It was not exactly running, but it was very much alive.

"Quick" I yelled, "the rat has just gone in under the fridge".

Harry came down with a murderous look in his eye and moved the fridge to one side, at which our opponent shot to the end of the verandah and disappeared under the very heavy washing machine which stands around the corner under the solar heater.

"Right, that's it", fumed Harry "we'll finish him once and for all".

He stormed off to the garden shed and came back with my old hockey-stick.

"I'm going to tilt the washing machine back towards me and, when it runs out, hit it. Just consider it's a hit from the edge of the D and give it all you've got".

I was not too happy at this idea but, when he said "think of the baby" my resolve strengthened. I gripped the familiar old stick and stood by, ready to send the rat into orbit over the hedge.

"OK, NOW" shouted Harry, and tipped the washing machine back towards him. Out came the rat, only it didn't play fair - it came out ducking and weaving like a prize fighter in training. I gave it all I'd got and the stick connected with the rockface instead of the rat, sending shockwaves up my arm, which nearly paralysed me, and sending the hockey-stick hurtling through the air towards Harry who, with one of his famous left-handed saves, reminiscent of his own hockey goal-keeping days, plucked it out of the air and whacked the, now disorientated, creature over the head, killing it outright. Shame really, Rozi would probably have loved that rat.

I did not mention this visitation up in the village in case they hot-footed it down with the Holy Smoke and cleansed us of the evil eye. We would probably have had a spray of olive leaves, previously taken to the church and dipped in Holy water, nailed to the front door as well. Religious rites, customs and superstitions are rife in countries all over the world, and Cyprus is no exception. The Holy Smoke and prayers to the most powerful saints take care of most things and, at the start of the New Year, the priest, wielding a bunch of leaves dipped in Holy water, visits all the houses in the village, entering every room and liberally sprinkling everything and everyone, in a ritual of blessing and purification. Recently, when David was once again visiting us, we were in a village a little way up in the hills, sitting one lunchtime enjoying a glass of the excellent red wine produced there. Opposite, in the church, the priest was making ready for a christening due to take place later that day. Not yet in his ceremonial robes, he was a picturesque sight in his faded robe with an old black turban wound round his head. Harry, always the artist, was dying to draw him. It is impossible to get a natural pose once the subject spots the camera or a sketch book, so Harry composes his picture first of all with his camera - usually from a bit of a distance with a telephoto lens. In this way he has captured the very essence of various

Not yet in his ceremonial robes.
Village Priest.

priests, monks, craftsmen and old people as they go about their daily business, in his magnificent line drawings. Sometimes I am sent in to assist in causing a subject to turn his head in a certain way, and today was easy, for I knew this priest well. Harry was able to get in some good shots as he explained to me the intricacies of the baptismal preparations. David, somewhat less initiated in the ways of the Greek Orthodox church, came across the road to join us and, on stepping from the bright sunlight outside into the cool, dim interior, got rather a shock when he was instantly hit over the head with a bunch of geranium leaves by the priest, who was getting a bit carried away by his own enthusiasm.

Sometimes it seems that superstition and religion become intermingled. Just down the road from here a right-angled turn takes the traveller to the Baths of Aphrodite, while, straight on, the road leads to Latchi. We turned left at this bend every time we went to the beach and one day we noticed, lying where the fourth road would lead, three or four dead baby goats. The following day there were one or two more. They did not appear to have been attacked by anything and, in any case, a fox would have carried them off. That night, when I went to get the mail from the coffee shop, I asked the *Mukhtar* to explain the mystery. He told me that the shepherdess, who cared for the large flock of more than a thousand goats roaming the territory around the Baths, firmly believed that, if she placed all the stillborn kids at a point where the roads made the sign of the Cross, her flock would be protected against the misfortune of other stillbirths.

I pondered on this and wondered if the practice had its roots in the sacrificial slaughter of animals for appeasement and had been handed down from Pagan times, when Aphrodite had been worshipped here. The Goddess, so prominent in the history and legend of this island, was born in a place of breathtaking beauty on the coast near the village of Kouklia, and her birth is enchantingly described by Homer in his Hymn 6.

The moist breeze of Zephyr brought her there on the waves of the sea with a noise of thunder amid the soft foam and the gold-clad Horae received her with joy. They decked her with precious jewels and set on her immortal head a beautiful crown of gold, and in her ears ear-rings of copper and gold.

Near where we live, a short distance away from the crossroads, are the legendary Baths of Aphrodite where, it is said, the Goddess bathed in seclusion, far away from prying eyes. A narrow path leads through trees and shrubs to a grotto, where a pool is fed by pure spring water trickling down the rockface. An ancient fig tree overhangs the scene and a beautiful maidenhair fern further enhances the magic of the place. In spring wild cyclamen bloom here in profusion and the air is filled with the scent of flowers and fragrant herbs. Childless women have long come here to hope and pray, for Aphrodite, or Venus, goddess of love, signifies fertility as well as great beauty.

Looking again at the tiny goats laid as an offering, I thought how naive this must seem to people from a more sophisticated world, but there is something very moving about the steadfast faith of a clear-eyed shepherdess.

CHAPTER 11

THE MAN FROM ATLANTIS

When we first came here to live the beach, which was little used even in summer, was always totally deserted in the early mornings and towards sunset. These were the times we went down to swim in the crystal clear water. The lack of development on this coast resulted in a beautifully clean beach, which stretched from a point of low white cliffs at one end, curving gently round for about a mile, to stop in an outcrop of rocks at the other. Beyond the rocks were small bays which were mainly pebbly and rocky but ideal for snorkeling. The coast went on round to the legendary Baths of Aphrodite, Fontana Amorosa and, finally, Cape Arnauti, the most westerly point of the island. At the furthermost end of the bay, from the white rocks, were two small establishments which served food and drinks to the occasional tourist in the summer season, but they were up off the beach on the escarpment above.

This was a veritable paradise. Golden sand, not the fine variety which clung to everything, but slightly heavier grains, which brushed easily off legs and feet and which, more importantly, made ideal nesting sites for sea turtles. From late May onwards we checked for turtle tracks on the clean sweep of sand and, later, saw where the hatchlings had clambered out, leaving tiny flipper marks on their way to the sea. Where possible, the eggs from some of the rarer green turtles were taken to the safety of the turtle hatchery at Lara, but numerous loggerhead turtles nested there and we could see that many of the hatchlings were managing to get past the first dangers they faced of foxes, land crabs and crows and reaching the sea. At the end of August the autumn migration began and we saw herons and egrets and, later, skeins of Siberian cranes winging over. In the early mornings, when we arrived at the beach, there would be a great flapping of wings as the ones resting on the rocks took off, circled a few times and dropped back again. As the air warmed up they began to get airborne and to circle overhead, slowly gaining height, until, suddenly, they would form into lines and fly off. One of the sounds I love most here is their harsh calling at night as they pass over our house on their way south.

One morning, in early summer, we went down to the beach as usual and were surprised to find that we did not have the place to ourselves. There was a battered wreck of a car at the bottom of the slope and a dilapidated, home-made contraption of a tent next to it. The proprietor of this was struggling at the water's edge with a basket of fishing nets and some empty plastic containers, obviously trying to lay the nets out to catch fish. He was not too successful at this and, the next morning, we saw him sitting on the white rocks with a fishing rod he had evidently cut from a piece of bamboo. As the weeks passed he erected various bits of wood, broken-down rattan and blankets and, in so doing, took up most of the parking space used by visitors. He even dug a small patch of the track and planted lettuce and spring onions! He was obviously intending to move in and live the life of a simple fisherman. A few worn-out chairs arrived, to be put on the beach with a rickety wooden table. This done, he went back to his mountain village to fetch his wife, for this was no local man from the Polis area. Once they had settled in, he covered his balding head with a white cotton hat and quickly adapted to his new way of life while she, a shapeless mass in a huge, flowered sun hat, brewed coffee for their guests or sat poring and mumbling over a large bible.

A trickle of tourists began to arrive and the new tenant had taken to leaping up and greeting them with "Ooh welcome!" and offering them coffee at the makeshift table. As this was the time before the trumpet blew and the Berlin Wall came tumbling down, West Berliners could take advantage of the eastern European airlines and, by crossing into East Berlin, fly to Cyprus for less than half the normal fare. Most of those arriving were young and female and tended to sunbathe without swimsuits. The term 'beachbum' took on a whole new concept. The coffee sessions were turning into free meals and, for this, he needed more fish.

One morning we arrived for a swim as usual, keeping well clear of the encampment. Something moving off-shore caught our attention and we gazed, dumbfound-ed. We were looking at the Man from Atlantis. He had on a bright blue snorkel mask sporting fluorescent orange twin tubes, fitted with balls at the end and, on his feet, he had a huge pair of black flippers. A large, black inflated inner-tube was around his waist and he was pushing in front of him another inner-tube, con-taining his basket of nets and floats. Like Poseidon, clasped in one hand he had something that looked like a toasting fork. Words alone are totally inadequate to describe this bizarre sight, but he did improve his catch. Gradually he became a permanent resident, walking the beach daily and fishing in the bay, and many people have enjoyed his hospitality.

One summer day, at the far end of the beach, we found a strange set of tracks. Made by a very large green tur-tle, the track measured more than a metre across. There was a flaw in the pattern and I recalled one of the Fisheries team telling me they had seen the irregular tracks of a big green on this beach and suspected it had one rear flipper missing, presumably bitten off by a shark when she left inshore waters for the deep sea. We followed the tracks to find she had dug a wide, shallow hole and then moved on across the beach to dig another. Sometimes turtles do move around like this, especially if they hit some rock, but this turtle had wandered erratically all over the beach, digging holes and not laying, until she had returned to the sea quite a long way from where she had come ashore. There were a lot of footprints around, for it was late July and many Cypriots were taking their annual camping holiday in the area. The confusing marks they left in the sand made the accurate reading of what went on rather difficult, but I knew that, if she had not jettisoned her eggs into the sea, she would be compelled to come out and try again the following night, so we decided to go down and look for her again.

By ten-thirty the beach was mainly quiet, most campers being asleep, but a group of men, sitting drinking coffee and enjoying the night air, called *"kopiaste"* to us. Vaguely translated, this traditional Cypriot greeting of hospitality means 'come and join us and share what we have'. We sat with them and the conversation turned to turtles. They had noticed tracks each morning and had, at first, assumed them to have been made by a tractor. I told them we were waiting for a big turtle that had been on the beach the previous night. They replied that, not only had they seen it, they had watched 'the man over there' photographing it at about seven o'clock that morning. I found this difficult to believe, for turtles do not normally stay ashore until daylight. They were adamant, however, that this one had. She did not appear while we were there that night so, the next day, I casually dropped by the encampment and asked the Man from Atlantis if he had seen a big turtle with one rear flipper missing.

"Ha", he replied, "it's very strange, but there are TWO turtles like that. Two days ago I saw one with the left flipper missing, but look at this picture I took last year, this turtle has the right flipper missing".

He rummaged in a box and brought out a photograph album, proudly displaying a snapshot he had taken with a flash. He detached it from the album and gave it to me (I still have it to this day). I was horrified at his complete lack of understanding, for the turtle was upside down. It was a big Chelonia Mydas which had been deliberately turned over on its back to prevent it from leaving the beach. Its left rear flipper was missing. In this position turtles are helpless and unable to move and, if left for any length of time, will develop breathing difficulties and certainly die. He then showed me another photograph he had taken. This was of a loggerhead turtle straining towards the sea while, astride it, sat a small fair-haired child.

Later that summer he found himself with a problem. He was asked by the local authorities to move. He did - a hundred metres up the sloping cliff, where he set up camp above the white rocks and carried on as before. He then hit another snag. There are plans to build a five-star hotel on this site and he had to leave there too. Unbelievably, he moved lock, stock and inner-tubes to the far end of the beach, where he dug in at the top of a low cliff and resumed his peripatetic way of life.

The mutilated turtle did not appear again that summer but, the following year, in June, I saw the unmistakable tracks where she had been digging all over the beach. I knew she would be back in a couple of weeks and, being keen to confirm the theory as to why she never actually laid her eggs, we decided to go down and look for her. The first night's watch brought no turtles at all ashore. The second night we were in luck! It was a Thursday, the day the Man from Atlantis always went back to his village for the night. The beach was deserted and the moonlight glistened palely on a calm sea. There was no sound save for the gentle surge and hiss of the waves on the sand. Harry, having agreed to accompany me with his photographic gear, had patrolled the beach one way

This was the turtle we had come to find.
Mutilated Turtle.

while I went the other and we were now sitting, motionless, on a big rock. Suddenly and silently, within a few metres of us, the surface of the water broke and the moon reflected on the carapace of a large turtle. She waited awhile, unmoving, at the water's edge, then began laboriously dragging her huge body up the beach. She passed us and started her first dig about eight metres or so away from where we were perched. We could see her clearly in the moonlight - there was only a foreshortened stump where the left rear flipper should have been. This was the turtle we had come to find. Down she went, lower and lower, as she threw out sand with her powerful front flippers. Then came the sad moment of truth, she could not dig out the underlying damp sand, for the deeper part of the nest that would contain the eggs, with one rear flipper missing. The stump moved futilely and, after a while, the poor creature moved on to dig again with her front flippers and fail again with the rear. In this manner she wandered over the beach for hours until, finally, she returned to the sea to jettison her eggs. She is doomed to continue with this pattern of life. Her instinct to reproduce herself is so strong, she will carry on her heartbreaking quest until she dies. She has no choice.

Soon after this incident we decided to take a few days off and, having been invited by the Fisheries Department, we packed up the jeep and headed across the Akamas peninsula to the turtle hatchery at Lara, where an Italian film crew had been making a film of the breeding turtles. Most of the stages had been filmed, but they still needed a sequence of a green turtle actually depositing eggs in the nest hole. We were equipped with walkie-talkie radios to keep in touch, so that whoever spotted a turtle could summon the others to bring all the equipment. Harry had decided that a scientific approach might be beneficial to the occasion and, with the Director of Fisheries' approval, had brought some nightsight binoculars from Akrotiri. He took himself off to Lara One to sit in isolated splendour with his high-tech aid to seeing turtles at night. You could see quite clearly with them, albeit everything was bathed in an eerie, green glow.

Once in position, he radioed back to base "OK, I'm in position at the top of the beach. Nothing, I repeat nothing, can come out of the sea without me seeing it".

The rest of us settled down back at base camp, playing cards and taking it in turns to patrol the other stretch of beach. There was nothing happening at our end and, after several hours, Harry called in "Negative on this beach, I'm coming in for a brandy".

He gathered up his radio and state-of-the-art nightsight binoculars and started back to camp, only to fall over a turtle twenty metres or so from where he had been sitting. She had been out, laid her eggs and was on her way back to the sea. Somewhat chastened, he called in with this rather depressing news before carrying on, only to fall over another one almost immediately. An agonized wail of despair came over the radio.

"Quick, there's another one here and I don't know if she's finished or not, she's just keeping perfectly still".

At this, the rest of us loaded up the gear and set off, only to hear Giorgos, who was patrolling our area, call in to say he had a big green at the top of the beach, but she was wandering about and did not look set to lay. Decision time and the boss said, "OK we'll go for Harry's".

We clambered through the rocks and hurried, Indian file, to his position, just in time to see the turtle throw the last lot of sand over her nest and start back to the sea. To this day, Harry doesn't know whether he dozed off, or whether the turtles managed to sneak out while he was scanning the other end of the beach.

Giorgos' turtle went back into the sea, without digging a nest, and we eventually turned in for a couple of hours sleep. My bed was under a rattan shelter about a hundred metres or so from the water's edge, and, climbing into a sleeping-bag, I was soon lulled to sleep by the rhythmic crashing of the surf. The early morning sun on my face woke me and, rolling over, I was mortified to see, right beside my bed and within easy touching distance, a set of tracks made by a very large green turtle. This was the one Giorgos had seen at the top of the beach and, again, she had been out and not laid her eggs. Happily, she returned the following night and the filming was completed.

After a cup of tea and the first swim of the day, we walked along the water's edge to check on any tracks that might have appeared once we had gone to bed. Reaching a small lagoon where the heavy surf of the previous night had subsided, leaving an expanse of crystal clear water over coarse, pink sand and flat, pink rock, Harry indicated that he wanted me to sit on the rock so that he could take some photographs. I was sitting with my bare feet in the water when I suddenly felt something touch my toes. I hurriedly moved my legs back up on the rock and saw a beautifully camouflaged octopus slowly swim back under a ledge, its tentacles streaming behind it. Each time I put my legs back in the water, the octopus came out and tried to grasp my foot. Harry's theory was that it was mistaking the pale pink nail varnish I was wearing for a shellfish. My theory was that, if I put my foot back in again, it was going to mistake me for its breakfast. As usual, I was urged not to be a baby, a little thing like that wouldn't hurt me. (I have noticed that he always seems to make these terse observations when he is safely behind the camera and I am in the firing line). However, not wishing to be dubbed a coward, I bravely replaced my legs in the lagoon and the octopus came out with astonishing speed and firmly grasped my foot. I hastily swung my

A beautifully camouflaged octopus.
Octopus.

legs up and it fell back into the water, with all its tentacles splayed out, like a parachute descending. I decided that, by now, it must be getting annoyed, not to mention hungry, and I was very wary of the sharp beak it had for cracking shellfish.

"One last time" pleaded Harry, who had forgotten all about his original idea and was concentrating on taking some close-up shots of the octopus. I sighed and replaced my legs in the water, only to snatch them sharply up on to the ledge again as the thing streaked out at an amazing rate of knots and, clambering up out of the water, flapped and slithered after my foot. At this point I beat a very hasty retreat and even the indomitable Harry was stunned into silence for once. He has some beautiful slides of that octopus in the lagoon though.

CHAPTER 12

IT'S ALL GREEK TO ME

From an English point of view Greek is a very difficult language to master, but I determined to learn to speak it colloquially so that I would be able to communicate with the people in whose country we had come to live. I have, more or less, managed to do this, albeit somewhat ungrammatically, and these endearing people never mind when I massacre their learned tongue - in fact my fractured Greek is a source of great merriment and knee-slapping in the coffee shop, when I go to collect the mail, or in the building supply shop, when I don't know the technical name of something Harry has asked me to buy. I am bombarded on all sides with helpful suggestions, which generally have nothing at all to do with what I am looking for, but the builders all have a great time, sometimes getting into heated arguments on my behalf until, at last, they all run out of ideas. Then Giorgos, who owns the shop, will quietly say in Greek, "Now, Sheila, tell me", and, with a bit of poetic descriptiveness, I always manage to get what I came for. Some of my attempts to describe things are obviously going to be preserved in local folklore. Toothless farmers are still convulsed with mirth, in the agricultural co-operative, when they recall the time I went in to buy some slug pellets. "Slug" not being a word that features largely in my Greek vocabulary, I was getting nowhere and being offered everything, from sulphuric acid to strychnine, to kill this mysterious pillager of my flowers.

"You DO know it" I said desperately. "It's the same as a snail but it hasn't got the little round house on top".

I have never understood why they found this so hilarious, but it seems that a bit of a quiz, early in the morning, brightens up their day. What they really appreciate, though, is when Harry comes along, for, despite my probably knowing the exact word we need, he will be encouraged to draw the desired object. This he does in true Rolf Harris fashion - a wheelbarrow starts off with a wheel (prompting all kinds of ridiculous suggestions), then he adds the handles, then the legs, until it only needs one or two strokes of the pen to show the finished article. Delighted shouts follow as they recognize the familiar object, and I always feel as though we should have provided a prize for the first one to get it. Shopping was never this much fun in England.

More erudite Cypriot friends correct my mistakes and explain grammatical errors but, in the village, where a strong dialect is spoken and many words will never be found in a dictionary, any failure to comprehend, on my part, instantly results in a repetition at full bellow, the speaker obviously convinced that, shouted loudly enough, the meaning will eventually become clear. Fortunately, I like languages and perseverance has meant that I can talk with the older residents, when we visit some of the more remote villages, and learn of life there in the past.

Families, it appears, were large and had to be completely self-sufficient, gleaning a hard living from the soil or the sea. Today, while most villagers are still mainly self-sufficient, keeping chickens, rabbits and pigeons for meat and growing their own vegetables, fewer families keep sheep and goats. Modern transport means it is less trouble to buy things like dairy products from the local shop. Almost all the women in the villages, however, make their own bread for the big religious festivities at Easter and Christmas, the bread-making often becoming a communal event, with several neighbours working together to fire up the big, out-

Varvarou, who lived in Kouklia.
Varvarou.

door bread ovens and form the dough into its traditional shapes.

One such village woman, whom we had known for many years, was Varvarou, who lived in Kouklia, where the remains of the temple of Aphrodite stand. This village was formerly the centre of worship of the Goddess, near the place where she was said to have emerged from the sea, and many of the treasures that have been unearthed there over the years, are housed in a small museum. Varvarou's brother, Giorgos, was the custodian of this museum and, one day, we were summoned to her house with the news that he had died. We expressed our sympathy and, in reminiscing, recalled the day, back in the nineteen seventies, when we had been in the village coffee shop with Varvarou, Giorgos and two off-duty policemen. Two children had come running down the road shouting that they had found a picture in the field, where they were tending the family goats. We all got up and followed them and, there, in the long grass where it had lain hidden for hundreds of years, was a square paving stone on which was depicted a perfect mosaic of Leda and the Swan. It was carefully transported to the museum where Giorgos washed it and the beautiful colours glowed brightly in the sunlight, as fresh as when they had been put there by the ancient craftsman. It was another of those incredible moments to remember, in this land so steeped in history and legend.

Some years later that same stone was to be stolen from the museum at Kouklia, on behalf of a wealthy and dishonest European. Happily, Interpol recovered the mosaic, unharmed, and it is now housed in the main museum in Nicosia, where security measures are more stringent.

We sat remembering all manner of things in Varvarou's tiny house, with the stone-flagged floor cool beneath

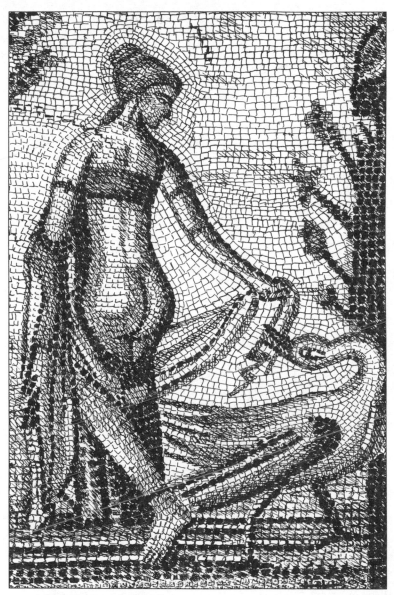

A perfect mosaic of Leda and the Swan.
Mosaic of Leda and the Swan.

our feet and chickens wandering in from the yard as the shadows lengthened. We sipped our *spajia*, or sage tea, for Varvarou was not only given the highly respected title *Hadjina*, meaning she had made the pilgrimage to the Holy Land and been baptized in the river Jordan, but she was well-versed in the healing power of herbs and in traditional cures for general ailments. Seeing that Harry had an aching back, she decided that the *venduza* were called for. These are little glass jars and the principle of their use is the same as the old fashioned cupping formerly practised in England.

She made him remove his shirt and lie, face down, on the bed. Then on the table she laid out four *venduza*, a cupful of *zivania*, a fork, some cotton wool and a candle, which she lit. She wrapped the cotton wool around the prongs of the fork, dipped it into the *zivania* and set it alight from the candle flame, before putting it into the *venduza* for a few seconds. Each time blowing out the flame on the fork, she placed the little glass jars on his back, where they stuck firmly in place. Once all four *venduza* were in position, she kept up a swift pattern - removing each glass jar in turn, heating it up again and replacing it in a slightly different position. When she was satisfied, she removed all four *venduza*, leaving him looking as though he had a case of giant measles, with circular red marks all over his back. She then poured what was left of the *zivania* over the area and massaged it thoroughly. His verdict? Felt good, but thought it would probably be less painful to let a couple of Japanese massage girls walk all over him.

Once back in our own village we told Theodosis about this cure for backache and he, somewhat disgruntledly, said that, for his money, she wouldn't be half as good as his wife at it, and pulled open a drawer which was full of *venduza*. We hastily changed the subject and asked him to tell us more of the time of his youth. Out came the bottle of ouzo, to be sipped and savoured with slices of *halloumi, angourakia* and bread, and, beneath the dappled green canopy of the mulberry tree, we settled on carved wooden chairs with their seats of woven straw. A baby goat nuzzled my hand expectantly, setting aquiver its silken, floppy ears, before dancing away on stiff legs to torment its mother. Brown hens scratched in the earth and four or five purring cats, backs arched and tails held stiffly upright, came to wind themselves around our legs. We were sitting comfortably, so he began.

When he was a boy, Theodosis recounted, he would ride down through our valley, on the way to his father's fields, and would see francolin, quail and chukar in large numbers. Now, with forty-five thousand licensed hunting guns on the island and modern, 4-wheel drive vehicles, capable of getting here quickly from the towns, their numbers have been decimated. Pesticides and insecticides do not help either. We feel privileged to have one pair of golden orioles returning to our garden every year, but Theodosis told us that in May, as he rode by, the valley would be filled with them, "like so many yellow fruit in the trees" he said. At night when they were passing through late, having been to the olive press, he recalled his fear at the thought of the large snakes they might encounter. Today, unless they are lucky (or unlucky, depending on their point of view!), visitors to Cyprus will never see a snake - reptiles preferring a wild habitat with no people around.

He told us of huge Griffon vultures soaring above the village, and how dead or dying animals would be nudged over the cliff to drop into the valley below, where they would be picked clean by the vultures. Now, apart from those Griffons which are protected and fed inside the British Sovereign Base at Episkopi, their numbers are very limited indeed. Those left in the Akamas area fly to Turkey (only forty miles across the sea from here) to feed and the few other nest sites in the Paphos region are closely monitored by the Game Department and the Ornithological Society. The programme of poisoning for rats, carried out over the years by the Department of Agriculture, has also taken its toll of vultures and other birds of prey that feed on rodents. The majestic Griffons no longer spiral above the village, watching and waiting for carrion to rip and tear with their formidable beaks until only the bones are left to bleach white in the scorching sun. Today carcasses must be buried, lest they rot where they lie.

What changes our old friend had seen in his lifetime. We sat in silence as the pearly luminescence of the Akamas twilight bathed the old stone house and Theodosis' head began to nod, then, slipping quietly away, we left him to his memories.

The birds, of course, face other life-threatening situations as well as those presented by snakes, cats, poisoning and old age. On winter Sundays we tend to keep our heads down as war is waged against the feathered population by the sporting fraternity. Although keen on competitive sport, I am, admittedly, not an admirer of blood sports. I can't quite see where the sporting challenge lies in blasting a songbird with a gun big enough to kill a horse. Whether it is foxhunting, bullfighting or shooting birds, the odds always appear to be heavily stacked in favour of *homo sapiens*. To be fair, I suppose there is sometimes an element of risk involved. The gentleman riding to hounds may fall off his horse and break his neck, or the matador be gored by a bull, but I would have thought the chances of a Mediterranean hunter being pecked to death by an enraged thrush must be pretty remote. Nevertheless, at daybreak on the appointed day, behind every bush there lurks a hunter, dressed to kill, in camouflaged combat gear and criss-crossed bandoliers. Twelve bore at the ready, fearless and alert, he plunges headlong into hostilities with the enemy. He gives no quarter, takes no prisoners,

A beautifully marked chukar walked in.
Chuck.

and, as a result, the pursuers now outnumber the pursued. The solution to this exigency has been a programme of rearing chukar to release into the wild at the start of the hunting season. These birds are ringed to see how far they manage to get before they are shot. One day, sitting on the front verandah, I noticed something fly low over the bushes and land in the road outside the front gate. I reached for the binoculars and watched, as a beautifully marked chukar walked in and wandered along the path under the orange and lemon trees. He stopped for a dust bath in the loose earth beneath the trees then ambled on to the birdbath where he fluttered up for a drink, looking an incongruous sight among the smaller songbirds. He was a regular visitor for several weeks, showing no fear of us. We could see that he had been ringed, so, presumably, he was used to human voices where he had been reared. The first Sunday of the winter hunting season opened up, like world war two, and we never saw Chuck again.

During the hunting season we would often find dogs abandoned here. Not properly trained, they were more of a hindrance than an asset to their masters and some of the less scrupulous hunters would simply drive home and leave them to their fate. The poor beasts would be left trying to fend for themselves in the wild and, in the end, would invariably fall prey to the poisoned meat, left out by the shepherds, for the foxes.

One day, when we were still in the poultry farming business, we had opened the door to the chicken run and the hens were pecking away organically in the orchard outside. It was approaching mid-day when we heard an appalling noise, and, dashing downstairs, we found a big splodge of blood and some white feathers in the road. We were easily able to follow the trail of blood and feathers down the track to an almond grove, where we found what was left of one of our hens. Its throat had been torn out and most of it had been devoured. We spotted the culprit, an abandoned hunting dog, looking guiltily round the edge of a large metal barrel, turned on its side, where the poor creature was obviously holing up. It growled and bared its teeth as we tried to approach and, Alfons having arrived, the three of us managed, with a bit of chicanery, to upend the barrel and trap the dog inside. We placed a very heavy stone on top, so that it could not escape, and went back to the house to telephone the police. They immediately offered to come and shoot it, but said it might take some time as they didn't have a gun. Several hours later, someone from the vet's office came to remove it and we thankfully led him down to where it was securely bottled up. When we got there the barrel was still in place with the stone on top, but there was a large hole scraped in underneath and the dog was gone. We kept the chickens in the next day and saw no signs of the stray, so, assuming it to be miles away by then, we let them out again. The following day it ate another one of our hens. We then had to keep them in the enclosure all day and they did not appreciate this at all - neither did we, because it created a lot of extra mucking-out. The situation was resolved shortly afterwards when the dog ran off with a chicken in the village. This time, the owner of the unfortunate bird tracked the culprit down and shot it.

CHAPTER 13

THE BEST OF BOTH WORLDS

As time passed we grew to know, and to better understand, the local people. Hardworking and enterprising, the Cypriot has a natural dislike of rules and regulations and he has a fool-proof way of dealing with them - he ignores them. Few are the Cypriot drivers who will use a parking meter when there is still room to park on the pavement or block a few exits, and, as for building regulations, if the local authorities put a demolition order on all illegal buildings, half of Cyprus would be torn down. The Cypriot is not a thief. If you lose your wallet you are likely to get it back intact, money untouched, but watch out in any business transaction - here it is very much a case of *caveat emptor*! The very mention of taxation causes near apoplexy. It amounts to grand larceny by the government and should be studiously avoided where possible. The bartering system thrives. Goods are traded for other goods and *Ah sto kalo* with VAT! The simple logic of the Cypriot peasant sees no justice in someone demanding a share of the profit when they have had no share in producing the goods. Friendliness and hospitality are his forté but, make an enemy of him, and you will have one for life. It causes him almost physical pain to part with his money, and, as we had seen so many times during the building of our house, he will never waste money on unnecessary equipment if there is something already available that will do the job. He is brilliant at improvisation. Take someone who makes wine, for instance. Not for him the special thermometers, sterilization tablets, air-locks and so forth - he likes to keep things simple.

One day we were sitting in a village coffee shop trying out some of the red wine they had produced from their own vineyards. Harry was extremely enthusiastic about this, telling me that it was pure, healthy stuff, which was full of iron and didn't have additives in it like most other beverages. He was on his third glass and happily munching some bread and *halloumi*, when I said I could hear water running.

"No" said the lady of the establishment, "that is my husband making this year's wine".

Harry leapt to his feet.

"There you go" he said "we can actually see it being made straight from the vines".

In the little yard at the back, where a few hens pecked away in the dust and a large, black pig was tethered, there was a tin bath standing against the wall underneath a drainpipe. The sound I had heard was grape juice coming down the drainpipe (presumably cobwebs and all) into the bath. Looking up we saw the *kafejis* with his trousers rolled up and shoes and socks removed, stoically stomping around in another tin bath which was up on the flat roof. This one was full of beautiful black grapes and, evidently, had a hole in the bottom so that juice could flow down the drainpipe to be collected in the other bath. You have to admire enterprise like this, and we did. We took a bottle of last year's brew home with us - cobwebs and all.

For his own children, the Greek Cypriot will spare no expense. Family ties are strong. They cherish their offspring and, unlike the United Kingdom, where baby-sitting services flourish, children are included in all family activities. If the adults are going to a restaurant to eat, the children go along too and no one minds if they are noisy or boisterous. When a small child gets drowsy or the baby falls asleep, there is always a spare pair of arms to cradle the infant. Most parents are prepared to give up everything to help their children. Grandmothers look after babies while mothers go out to work, managing their own chores and then probably cooking the evening meal for the whole family at the end of the day. They strongly believe in education to give their children a better chance than they had, and will, themselves, live a completely simple life in order to save the money to give them this chance. Thus, many, who had no more than a basic education at a village primary school, now have sons and daughters who are qualified doctors, lawyers, teachers and architects. Others start their children off in their own businesses, and girls are virtually assured of a dowry house when they marry.

In the village the elderly are not pushed into retirement homes as they become unable to look after themselves - the family will care for them. Old people are a natural part of the community and their standing is not diminished by the fact that their working days are over. I once saw an old shepherd, frail and scarcely able to walk, being greeted by his sons when they visited the village for a family celebration. Each, in turn, kissed the old man's hand and touched it to his forehead as a mark of filial respect.

It is truly a community where they share in each other's lives. When there is a wedding, there is no guest list to be pruned to the bone, everyone is invited, and, when someone dies, all the villagers will call at the house of the bereaved to offer their condolences. These warm and hospitable people have accepted us into their midst and we share in their celebrations and, sometimes, their sorrows. If we can help with specific problems, we do, be it taking olives to the press, or sick people to the little hospital, when there is no taxi available.

They are proud people too, and sometimes quite rigid in adhering to certain forms of social conduct. Early one morning, as we were getting ready to go to Paphos, I heard someone shouting outside and looked out of the window to see an old couple from the village going up the lane on their donkeys. The husband, riding in front, was holding the rope of the second animal on which his wife was slumped over, crying noisily. They had been on the way to their fields to pick olives. He had been walking, leading the first donkey, which had a heavy, wooden ladder roped to its back. There had been some rain in the night and the donkey had slipped, while negotiating a steep bend, and the ladder had swung round knocking the old woman, who had been riding side-saddle, to the ground. I shouted to him to put her in the car and we would go straight to the hospital, but they continued doggedly up the track, adamant that they had to go home first. I followed them up to their house where, despite being badly shocked, bleeding from a head wound and unable to stand upright, she insisted on changing from the clothes she had been wearing in the fields, to some she considered more suitable for a doctor to see. Everything she had on was spotlessly clean, but I had to get her into her Sunday best from the skin out before she would let me take her to the hospital for x-rays and treatment. Ever since that day, she has called me her daughter and, indeed, treats me like one. By some miracle she sustained no serious injury, and, although well past her seventieth birthday, was back in the saddle again in a matter of weeks.

Harry was once driving up out of the village in the mini-moke on his way to collect stones for landscaping. Some considerable way past the last house, he came across old Marika, collapsed in the hot sun at the side of the road. She was conscious, but in pain and unable to get up. He gently lifted her into the car and drove back to her house, where he gave her some water and laid her on the bed. Not being able to understand her fully and with the village deserted, for the carobs were being harvested, he came down to fetch me. She told me she had a chronic back condition and needed an injection. I took her to the hospital and was then despatched to find her sister, wife of the local chemist, to look after her. A week or so later I heard someone calling my name outside the house and there, leaning on a stick, stood old Marika, having struggled all the way down from the village to bring me some fresh eggs.

Unusually, for a Cypriot, she had no children of her own. Her husband, a much-respected man in his nineties and, formerly, a primary school teacher, still drove an ancient green tractor to his fields. Sitting proudly upright, with a straw trilby hat set squarely on his head, he used to trundle through the village at a steady two or three miles an hour and we affectionately called him Stirling Moss.

Some months later I was on my way through the village when I saw a crowd, with sombre faces, gathered outside their house. "*Ela kori*", come daughter, they called, so I went in to find the old man laid in a simple coffin on the table, his face covered with lace cloths and sprigs of fragrant rosemary. The women were sitting around with Marika while friends and neighbours came to offer their sympathy. I was motioned to a chair in the circle of women and cautioned that I must not sit with crossed legs. After a while, one of the women began to chant the praises of the dead man, then another took it up, until Marika, rocking to and fro, joined in and ended with "*ah ton andra mou*", oh my husband, at which everyone burst into tears and loud wailing. This sequence was repeated over and over as they shared and expressed their grief.

The *myroloyia*, or singing of dirges for the dead, is mediaeval in origin, dating from the 12th or 13th century, and the singing is always done by women. Today it has almost ceased to exist in Cyprus, and, when the last of the praise singers has passed on, this ancient art, too, will be lost forever.

That same afternoon, after a packed ceremony at the church, the old teacher was buried, the villagers all linking arms abreast behind the coffin to escort him through the village street to the burial ground.

The following spring, Harry and I were in the mountain region of Paphos, not far from the lovely old monastery of Chrysoroyatissa, as usual looking for old churches, people and buildings to draw. We came to a signpost which indicated a village both to the left and the right of the road. Electing to turn left, we came to a fairly modern village on the top of a plateau. With nothing old or ethnic to interest Harry as an artist, we retraced our steps to the signpost, realizing that the old, uninhabited, village must lie below the main road. Following the other sign, we soon found ourselves in a deserted village. Harry was quickly engrossed in photography and sketching, while I wandered around the crumbling old buildings. I saw a movement in the shadows and slowly, one by one, half a dozen black-clad old people emerged from various doorways. They were curious to know where we were from and smiled delightedly when I told them where we lived.

"Do you know Moussolitis?" they asked.

This was the real name of Stirling Moss and I told them he had died some months earlier. They were visibly upset at this news, for he had been the teacher at the village school there for many years and they were all former pupils of his. What news of his wife, Marika? I was plied with questions and then stories, as they sat on a low wall in the warm sunshine, recalling their youth and telling me what life was like then. They said they preferred to spend their remaining days in this beloved, familiar village, derelict as it was, rather than move to a strange new environment. We left with messages and greetings for Marika (which I duly delivered) and the feeling, once again, of the closeness and comradeship of these old village communities.

Here we have the best of both worlds, for, on the one hand, we have the warmth and companionship of the village people and many other Cypriot friends, while, on the other, our secluded house offers us privacy and peace when we are alone and a beautiful setting for the many lunch, dinner and pool parties that take place with visiting family and friends. A week never goes by, particularly in the summer season, without several sets of visitors arriving from the UK or the British bases. These days are filled with laughter and reminiscences, eating and drinking, sunning and swimming, sometimes to the accompaniment of music from the self-styled KEO TRIO, so called because of the vast quantities of the local KEO beer consumed on these occasions. The trio consists of Harry on cornet, the aspiring deep-sea diver from Droushia on soprano saxophone and our son, who is a professional drummer, busking on an ancient tuba, playing the washboard or hitting a variety of percussion instruments ad-lib. The noise? Well, our only neighbours are Helli and Alfons and they always join in anyway!

We often have people here for Christmas too, for this is a lovely place to spend the festive season. If you want a traditional white Christmas, there is usually plenty of snow on Troodos by then and, if you don't want to ski, the scenery is breathtaking in itself. In either case, at the end of the day when the temperature drops even lower, you can gather round a roaring fire of pine logs and drink the Forces' favourite *gluhewein*, red wine heated with cinnamon, spices and brandy. They say you need to hold your glass with a napkin, or it may become so hot you will burn your fingers. Alternatively, you can add more brandy and you won't feel the pain.

Music from the self-styled Keo Trio.
The Keo Trio.

We prefer to spend the festivities here in the warm sunshine. On Christmas Eve we move around to wish various friends and neighbours a Happy Christmas and Harry takes his cornet to play traditional English carols. At midnight there is a service in the village church and our sweet-faced priest, Papa Kyriacos, welcomes everyone with his lovely smile. On Christmas morning people come and go and we offer drinks by the pool, where the poinsettia tree spreads its blazing, scarlet bracts. Whether we are alone for the occasion or not, we always cook a traditional Christmas lunch with turkey and plum pudding and then exchange telephone calls with family and friends in far-off lands. During the afternoon Calliope's grandchildren, who are in the village for the Christmas holiday, come chattering down the lane, the eldest girl carrying a recorder and the youngest boy clutching a bedraggled bunch of daisies he has picked on the way. They file upstairs to the living-room and lustily sing carols for us. Harry, with a straight face, sometimes accompanies them on the huge tuba, causing the whole choir to collapse in helpless giggles. Fortified with boxes of chocolate, they go off up the track waving and shouting *"Kala Christougena"*, Happy Christmas, and the day is brighter for their having been here.

Sometimes, at this time of the year, we have really spectacular electrical storms. The view from our house across the bay is ever changing and always beautiful, and, during a violent storm, it is no exception. The sky looms black as ink and the sea is whipped up into white horses, which come in along the shore in long rollers, reminding me of Perranporth in Cornwall. Vivid forks of lightning split the sky, seeming to stand on top of the mountains. At times this electrical discharge is a lovely violet colour against the deep black of the sky, and round and round is the incessant roar and crash and rumble of thunder. When it rains, water pours from the lowering clouds in a deluge and our dried-up stream-

The poinsettia tree spreads its blazing scarlet bracts.
Poinsettia Tree.

bed becomes a raging torrent. On occasions, the wind blowing from the wastes of Siberia, sweeps across Turkey, whips up the water in the bay and slams into the front of the house with a vengeance that sends us rushing to wind down the big storm shutters and retire inside. Sometimes, in its wake, it leaves a frosting of snow on the peaks of the mountains opposite, and, as the turbulence it created in the bay gradually subsides, the water near the shore is left with a fine suspension of sand, so that the sea turns to an opalescent aquamarine, fringed with the frothing white of breaking waves.

One winter (actually it was the day before Christmas Eve), it was dry and sunny, but with a rough sea and an exceptionally strong wind blowing. We were sitting by a blazing log fire when, looking out of the big windows, we noticed a pink mass in the bay, close to the shore. With the always-handy binoculars, we saw that it was a large flock of flamingos milling about to and fro. The salt lakes at Akrotiri and Larnaca are home to the flamingos in winter, but they never appear on this side of the island. These must have been aiming for one or the other of the salt lakes and been unable to get up over the mountains on their usual migratory route because of the strong headwind, or because they were already too exhausted having struggled against the wind on their journey. We watched them for more than ten or fifteen minutes, as they flew to and fro in a disordered way. Then, abruptly, one bird, seeming to make a decision, turned and started to fly parallel to the coast towards Cape Arnauti. The other birds, flying in formation behind, followed as it led them, low over the water, past the highest point to cross over to the other side of the peninsula, at a place where the mountains let down into the sea and they did not have to get to any great height. They must then have followed the south coast up to one of the salt lakes.

I have always loved all kinds of wildlife but never realized, before we came here to live, just how large a part wild birds would play in our lives. They are a never-ending source of joy. We even have Christmas robins, as familiar and friendly as the ones in the gardens at home, singing sweetly and landing on the verandahs in the hope of crumbs dropped from the tables. The female redstart spreads her beautiful red tail in the stone birdbath and, at night, she will roost inside the front porch, sheltered from any strong winds that may blow in from the sea. I once read somewhere that, in mediaeval times, Cyprus was given the title THE SWEET LAND. That it surely is.

CHAPTER 14

A BOXFUL OF OWLS

Every now and then we go on expeditions for Harry to gather material for his artwork. Sometimes we stay in the Paphos area, where there are many beautiful old Byzantine churches and monasteries. On other occasions we exchange houses for a few days with friends whose home is in Lania, a lovely, well-kept village just a few miles below Platres. From there we explore the different world of the mountains and find churches built with steeply-tiled roofs, and ancient monasteries tucked away in remote places. There are beautiful old villages with picturesque, narrow streets and houses overhung with wooden balconies.

Leaving here for Lania, we go up over the mountain and down into Paphos, then, taking the Limassol road, we soon turn left and drive up through the lovely Dhiarizos valley, passing through deserted Turkish villages and small Greek communities, until the road crosses the river bed and winds steeply up towards the little village of Ayios Nicolaos. The spectacular scenery makes the dodging of the odd tourist bus worthwhile. Huge, dark-windowed and air-conditioned, they speed along looking strangely out of place in this ancient environment. The only vehicles that dare to challenge these colossi on the narrow mountain roads, with their terrifying drops into the river bed below, are driven by the more cavalier of Cypriot taxi drivers, whose turn of speed in overtaking by instinct rather than sight, is unmatched in the annals of motoring history. Sometimes we pass the village bus on its way down to the market at Paphos. Leaving early in the morning, with children going to school

In the more remote villages they are dependent on their bus.
Village bus.

and villagers going to town, the bus will be carrying produce to sell, gas cylinders to be exchanged, sometimes carobs for the processing plant. All manner of things will be tied to the top or lashed on to the rear platform. Returning at lunchtime, it will carry bags of grain, fertilizer or cement - perhaps even a live pig or goat will be loaded up. On Sundays it will probably be carrying wedding guests, all decked out in their finery, or on a feast day, pilgrims to a particular monastery. In the more remote villages they are dependent on their bus and each one has the name of the village, and the District in which it lies, displayed on the front. They are generally painted a bright red and green and, happily, as they become unserviceable, many villages are opting to replace them with new ones of the same, traditional design rather than change to more modern, anonymous coaches.

Our first encounter with our own village bus took place only a week or so after we had come here to live. We had gone down to Latchi, to attend a big wedding party, and the bus had ferried the guests there in two or three batches, for cars were few and far between in those days. When we came to leave, sometime after midnight, the bus, having just been loaded up with its last lot of revellers, was a little way ahead of us on the road. It was a dark night, with no moon, and suddenly we saw Andreas, the bus driver, flagging us down. His lights had failed, but he had a simple and obvious solution. He followed our car, tucked in closely behind and using our headlights to see the road ahead - his busload of singing passengers quite unconcerned as we wound up the hill to the village, past the hundreds of feet drop into the valley below.

Now, as we pass the village buses on narrow stretches of road on our journey up to the mountains, we exchange greetings with the driver and passengers and accept an apple or pear, or whatever is in season, handed out of the window by these open, smiling people.

Thus we find hidden churches.
Hidden church.

Always there are the people, friendly and hospitable and curious to know where we are from. They are delighted when they discover we are able to communicate with them and are full of information about their area and the local customs. There is usually a cousin, brother, uncle or someone to take us to see this or that building or relic. Thus we find hidden churches that no tourist, however well-equipped with maps, will ever reach. If we are seeking out a particular church, they will summon the priest to unlock the door and show us its treasures. They will often mention another church nearby and, when we confess we have never heard of it, will elect someone to climb in the vehicle with us and show the way. If it is some distance from the village one or more of the women will scramble in, carrying candles and oil, glad of the chance to pay a visit to the church without having to toil through the fields in the heat. Sometimes we have discovered beautiful old churches in this way and, at other times, have been disappointed to find the building has been renovated in the past and looks dull and uninteresting. This happened on one occasion and one of the women casually mentioned that the very old church was 'down there'. Climbing 'down there', we found ourselves in a large cave, with the remnants of wall paintings still visible on the smoke-blackened walls. A huge altar was hewn out of the rock and above it was fixed a large wooden cross. This ancient church dates back to the fifteenth century and was discovered when the villagers were preparing fields for planting grape vines. It bears the name Chrysospiliatissa, Our Lady of the Golden Cave.

Before the Turkish occupation of the northern part of Cyprus, the monastery of Apostolos Andreas, situated at the very tip of the Karpas peninsula, was a place of pilgrimage for those who were sick, and huge, sculpted candles were taken there by the faithful seeking a cure. Greek Cypriots no longer have access to this very special place of worship and pilgrimage, so these candles are now placed in many of the island's other churches and monasteries. Made either in the image of the sick person, or that part of them which is afflicted, I have seen, amongst others, arms and legs, hands and feet, heads and hearts and, sadly, whole effigies of tiny babies. These are brought to the church of the saint renowned for taking care of their particular problem.

Tucked away in the Akamas peninsula, a long way behind our village, is a small church named Panayia tou Tyflou, the Holy Virgin for the Blind. The blind, and those with failing vision, make pilgrimages there, sometimes from great distances, to pray for the restoration of their sight. I have serious problems with my eyes, and, sometimes, old women from the village come to me bringing pieces of damp cotton wool which, when they have lit a candle and prayed for me, they have rubbed on the Holy Icon and the smoke-grimed walls. They gently smear this on my eyelids, leaving me looking like a rather surprised panda, yet strangely humbled and comforted by their simple faith.

The Cyprus government now has an excellent programme in progress to restore old churches and monasteries, and some of the beautiful wall paintings, which have survived the years of damp, candlesmoke and the ravages of Attila, are being restored with loving care.

From our Lania base we once visited an old uninhabited monastery at Kalopanayiotis. Travelling in October, through green pine forests and beech woods blazing with fiery autumnal tints, we went up through the Troodos mountains to Prodhromos, down through the picturesque villages of Pedhoulas and Moutoullas (where the pure spring water is bottled) and on to Kalopanayiotis. There, accessible by a weathered stone bridge across a ravine, stands the lovely old monastery of Ayios Yiannis Lambadistos. No monks live there now and we were disappointed to find that the door to the main church was locked. We were there for quite some time, drinking in the mellow beauty of the buildings while, with artistic talents in overdrive, Harry photographed and sketched contentedly. Suddenly I noticed the village priest approaching us across the bridge. Curious to know what was keeping us so long in the cloisters, he was delighted when he found we could understand him. When he learned how far away we lived, he apologized that the door had been locked. This was because of the process of restoration going on inside; however, he had a key and, withdrawing it from the pocket of his robe, he unlocked the heavy wooden door and pushed it open so that the bright sunlight flooded in. We stood there stunned by the magnificence of the wall and ceiling paintings, some done by the Italians in the most glorious blues. There were three churches, all built at different times, forming the main body of the monastery. The earliest dated back to the eleventh century and all three were covered by a single, steeply-sloping, tiled roof, built to withstand the heavy snowfall in winter. If you closed your eyes, you could almost hear the chanting of monks, from a long-ago age, instilling a strange sense of peace and tranquillity.

We left there refreshed and exhilarated by our experience and, as it had been a long time since breakfast, ravenously hungry. Over the mountain again and heading for Lania, we stopped at one of the trout farms just below Platres. Called Psilodhendron, Tall Tree, it is aptly named, being set among towering pine trees. Here we sat in the welcome shade, listening to the rushing and gurgling of the clear mountain stream as it splashed into the tanks where the rainbow trout swam. At Latchi we have superb fish but, that day, in the shadow of Mount Olympus, there was nothing to compare with the big oval platters presented to us on which lay a huge trout, brushed with olive oil and cooked to perfection over the charcoal. Accompanied by a fresh salad, local bread and a carafe of dry, white wine, this was indeed the food of the Gods.

Strangers visiting here often ask us what we find to do with ourselves all day. This invariably brings a wry smile to my face, for the fact is there are never enough hours in the day to complete all the tasks we have planned - this despite the early rising of Harry, who is always the first one up in the mornings and putting on the kettle for early morning tea before six o'clock. To begin with the garden is so big that, were we able to afford it, there would be plenty of work for a full time gardener. As it is we have to cope with it all ourselves. The same applies to housework, which I would opt out of with great delight if ever afforded the opportunity. In addition, Harry likes to spend as much time as he can in his studio and this, in itself, necessitates trips out into the field to gather material for his drawings. There are wild birds to watch, turtles and fruit bats to observe, spring flowers and orchids to study, friends to entertain and a book to write, not to mention a swimming pool to maintain. I like the early morning task of testing and cleaning the pool and fishing out the odd frog, toad or shrew which might have fallen in during the night. All kinds of interesting things are happening around me while I do this and it never seems to be a chore.

Most days seem to bring some fascinating event to cause us to stop whatever it is we are doing and stand, captivated, and watch. A few days ago, from the kitchen window, I saw Oscar suddenly streak across the dirt road outside and grab something. On closer inspection I could see that it was an unlucky chameleon, tightly clasped in the snake's jaws, with no chance of escape. Our roving reptile then went at a leisurely pace across the orchard and into the stream-bed, his head held high and clear of the ground, with the unfortunate chameleon destined to be his lunch.

love to find chameleons in the garden and see how these weird-looking creatures change, from grey or brown when they are on the ground, to a bright green as, in slow motion, they climb a shrub and get in among the foliage. Their strange, swivelling eyes, each working independently of the other, give them all-round vision and their long tongues whip out at lightning speed to grab a butterfly or fly and retract again. (It rather reminds me of those party blowers people seem to like aiming at each other on New Year's Eve). Their painfully slow, wobbling gait makes them easy prey for the likes of Oscar and, to add to their misery, the local people do not like them at all. They say the chameleon was entrusted with a message to deliver to Jesus that Judas was going to betray him but, because it was so slow, it did not get the message to him in time. Poor, maligned old chameleon, I like them anyway, and they are always welcome in our garden.

One day, when we were both busily working there, Harry called me over to see a rock lizard which was behaving strangely. It was lying, motionless, next to a stone, in a place where a shrub had recently been watered, and had scooped a hole partly in underneath the stone. Harry dived for his camera and we waited and watched as it slowly laid five or six elongated, oval eggs, pushed the earth in over them and left. We have some excellent slides of the eggs being laid in sequence.

On another occasion, when he was up on the roof replacing a couple of cracked tiles, Harry shouted to me to watch the road near the front gate. I hurriedly dropped the floor mop and reached the gate just as a large hawk flew past, only a few feet above the ground, with a white pigeon clutched firmly in its talons. The hawk was unable to gain much speed or height because of the weight of its prey, so I chased down the lane after it in the mini-moke to a point, just before our track

It slowly laid five or six elongated, oval eggs.
Lizard laying Eggs.

meets the main road, where the ground drops away, on the right hand side, into a citrus plantation leading to a steep-sided, wooded ravine. Here the hawk was able to glide down into the shelter of the trees and I was unable to see the end of the luckless pigeon. Later that day, I walked up to the village with some spare lettuce plants for Theodosis. As we sat in the shade of his mulberry tree, a flock of domestic pigeons wheeled overhead and drifted down into the field, where the birds began pecking busily away in the corn stubble.

"You'll never guess what happened this morning" said Theodosis, "I was coming out of the gate and a big hawk dropped out of the sky, snatched a pigeon and flew off with it!".

One day a kestrel almost made off with our male pied wheatear. The female kestrel circles our area at least three times a day and the birds go quiet as her shadow passes over the garden - you can almost hear the menacing music for Stephen Spielberg's film, JAWS, playing. This particular day, Piedy was perched on top of his favourite post, the electricity pole in the lower orchard, singing blithely away. We were watching him from the verandah when the kestrel, yellow talons extended, plummeted out of the sky straight towards him. With impeccable timing, Piedy whipped off the pole and dropped down into the orchard. A split second later the huge claws struck right where he had been, as the kestrel landed on the pole. These little dramas happen all the time and are a large part of the fascination of living here. Then, of course, there was our special Johnny.

One year the Scops owls had reared their young and two of the fledglings were safely away. The adult birds kept returning to the box at intervals, however, and we could hear that at least one chick was still inside. They stopped bringing it food, but carried on returning to the balcony and nearby pine trees, calling loudly, obviously

Then, of course, there was our special Johnny.
Johnny.

expecting it to leave the nest. When it did not respond, their visits dwindled and, eventually, they abandoned it. The following day we could still hear movement in the box and, when the adult birds did not return as dusk fell, we lifted out the remaining chick and discovered that it was deformed. It looked as though it had been squashed, with one wing and both legs being pushed to one side. Its body and head were perfect and it was completely unafraid.

The little owl looked at me and purred and I knew I had to try and save him. I thought perhaps, if we could straighten and strengthen his legs and exercise his wing, he might be able to join the others. First of all though it was obvious that he was very hungry indeed. I stole one of Harry's best sable paintbrushes and mixed up a mess of raw chicken liver and egg yolk. He grabbed wildly at this, almost swallowing down the brush, and, bit by bit, he consumed a considerable amount. I gave him some water to drink in the same way and, as I was holding him somewhere under my chin during this process, we both got in a horribly sticky mess. I cleaned him up with a toothbrush dipped in warm water, and gently brushed his feathers with another toothbrush to dry them. He did not object to this procedure at all, in fact it was fairly obvious that he liked it. Nestling in under my chin he made his little purring noise, turning his head this way and that, his beautiful yellow eyes not missing a thing.

We found a wicker basket, which had a handle, lined it with soft paper and some dried grass, then hung it up on a hook in the trellis underneath the nest box. We brought it inside when we went to bed, afraid something might attack him, but during the day he stayed there suspended in the basket, covered with a red and white checked cloth. Every time I spoke to him or he heard my voice, he would make his little purring sound.

I knew it was going to take a miracle but, if only I could get him to a point where he could fly and perch, I felt sure he would have a chance in the wild where he belonged. I don't know where the owls find their big slow-worms, but we didn't have much luck poking about in the sun-baked earth, so we became avid fly swatters and he had to make do with the egg and liver mix with the odd, fly, moth or beetle thrown in. He would eat whenever food was offered and always seemed to enjoy the subsequent grooming, purring away and never once struggling. Taking the advice of an ornithologist, I massaged his legs in warm water every day and gently tried to straighten them. We would close all windows and instigate flying lessons on the carpet, where he'd try eagerly and desperately to get airborne with his one good wing, but he only ever succeeded in going round in asymmetric circles.

I very soon realized that there was no way he would be able to survive in the wild and, despite my attachment to him, it was cruel to keep a nocturnal creature like this so restricted. I could not, however, bear the thought of putting him out of his misery. Johnny himself solved the problem. One day, struggling with his usual eagerness to get aloft, he suddenly came to a halt, bowed his head and the light slowly went out of his beautiful golden eyes. Harry carved a small tombstone and we buried him in the garden among the flowers and shrubs. I wept for days.

Now and then our lives are touched by sadness like this, but, more often, they are filled with laughter. Not long ago a visiting Wing Commander succinctly summed it all up. Having wined and dined well at Latchi, he was sitting on our front verandah, sipping a brandy, as the Johnnies whizzed to and fro overhead feeding their chicks. Looking up, he said "I say, you've got a boxful of owls, what a hoot!"

The owls are still with us, but things are inevitably changing as civilization catches up with us. Latchi which, ten years ago, consisted of a tiny harbour, one or two eating-houses and a lovely old stone carob barn, now has holiday apartments, shops, fish taverns and bars in plenty. The old stone barn has been turned into a restaurant and, next door to it, they have opened up a disco. We even have apartments in the village now. Old stone houses are being torn down to make way for more modern buildings and, as the older generation passes on and the last donkeys are replaced with tractors and Mercedes, the old way of life will be gone forever.

For now we are content to be part of what is still considered to be a backwater, far from the main towns, and to enjoy it as it is before too many people, coming here because they are so impressed with the wild, natural beauty of the place, move in and promptly start trying to change it.

The beach remains as lovely as ever, especially in the early mornings. The Man from Atlantis is still there, although the inner tubes have been replaced by a rubber dinghy with a small outboard motor, and various other caravans and awnings have sprung up in the field around his seaside residence. Migrating birds still land on the rocks, but there are fewer turtles now, the big green ones, in particular, need a dark deserted place to breed and are easily disturbed by bright lights and the noises made by people and dogs.

Only the wild Akamas itself remains unchanged, looking as it must have looked for thousands of years. Above the village, and a little way along the dusty track, there is a high place to sit and watch the incredibly beautiful sunsets. Behind is Chrysochous bay and, in front, a wide sweep of glittering sea on the southern side, from Ayios Giorgos and Lara to Tijoni and beyond.

Who knows what undiscovered archaeological secrets and treasures lie buried here still? This is Cyprus at its most imposing and magnificent.

I am unable to explain its magic, the pull that draws people back time and again. I only know that, much as I dearly love my homeland, I would rather live on this sun-kissed, sea-circled little island than anywhere else on earth.

GLOSSARY

*a*h t*o*n *a*ndra mou	oh my husband
alki*o*ne	kingfisher
angour*a*kia	small cucumbers
arg*a*ki	stream bed
bat*i*ha	watermelon
bouzo*u*ki	musical instrument
caveat emptor!	let the buyer beware!
Christ*o*s An*e*sti	Christ is Risen
*E*cho bat*i*hes	I have watermelons
*E*la k*o*ri	Come daughter
flao*u*nes	Cypriot Easter cakes
gluhewein	mulled wine
Hadjina	woman pilgrim to Holy Land
hallo*u*mi	Cypriot cheese
kafej*i*s	coffee shop proprietor
Kal*a* Christo*u*gena	Happy Christmas
Kal*i* m*e*ra	Good morning
Kalosor*i*sete	Welcome
kapnist*i*ri	incense burner
kl*e*ftiko	meat cooked in enclosed pot
kl*e*ftis	thief
kokkinelli	Red sweet wine
Kopi*a*ste	come and share my meal
koumpari	Best men
louk*a*nika	spicy sausages
lo*u*nza	smoked pork loin
matsik*o*ritha	small wild narcissi
m*e*spilia	loquat tree
metax*a*kia	little silk flowers
mezzes	mixed dishes/assortment of food
myrol*o*gia	dirges sung for the dead
niktok*o*rakos	fruit bat
*o*xi	no
Loulo*u*thia tou P*a*squa	Easter flowers
pist*o*la	hydraulic rock breaker
pith*a*ria	large wine/oil jars
p*o*mpa	pump
R*e*zzi	traditional wedding dish
sph*y*rnae	small barracuda
Ah St*o* kal*o*!	To hell with!
Tsakist*e*s	Cracked green olives
vend*u*za	cupping jars
vr*i*si	freshwater spring
zivan*i*a	alcohol distilled from grapes

EMERALD APHRODITE

*is well researched, with vivid and determined writings. The woven aspects of its storyline are masterly pieced together by **Roger Dawson**, and although fiction it is, however, written against the backcloth of factuality.*

Clare Spencer is to most of her country a truly remarkable young woman, fit in both mind and body. Aged only thirty-seven, she was the United Kingdom's second woman Prime Minister. No one had fought harder or campaigned more vigorously for peace than she throughout her life, but it was not until she decides on taking a week's secret and private holiday in the sunkissed but strifed Mediterranean island of Cyprus, that these very forces in the world against which she had fought so hard,
the inability to settle differences by peaceful means,
that will shatter her own personal world.
On her arrival in the idyllic Island of Aphrodite an
ex-university friend, Richard Rowland, awaits her. The taste of freedom is naturally revived. But as destiny has it things were not to happen as she had hoped...
Helena Haduanois has masterminded, operation, EMERALD APHRODITE, and Clare Spencer was chosen to play the key role, allowing no failure.

Helena as a child had lost her father who was killed by enemy's bullets when fighting for his country; at the age of twenty her lover is shot in similar circumstances. The final blow being the division of her country by an invading neighbouring country and at the same time the loss of her beloved brother. Twenty years later she decides that it is time to HIT BACK...

'A NOVEL WORTH READING'

Published by KYRIAKOU

CYPRUS
in colour

The Cyprus Magical Bestseller

226 photos, 128 pages

"As a gift for someone who knows the island, or indeed to intrigue those who do not, or merely to spoil oneself, "Cyprus in Colour" would be hard to better. It's a pictorial gem of a book that seeks to introduce its reader or transport him back to the warmth and magic of this Mediterranean island."

BOOK REVIEW EXTRACT from SUŃJET, the in-flight magazine of CYPRUS AIRWAYS

Published by KYRIAKOU

THE APHRODITE PLOT

by michael jansen

THE APHRODITE PLOT tells the story behind the headlines...

Between Easter and August of 1974, a series of events shook the island of Cyprus. The result was the division of this beautiful island, a great loss of life and 200,000 Greek Cypriots became refugees in their own country. This tragedy still lives on today.

"This is the story of the people of Cyprus whose lives were shattered by events not of their making and beyond their power to control."

Published by KYRIAKOU

The
PARADISE COLLECTION

by JOHN WATERHOUSE

Cyprus is a country of contrasts reflected on its people. They are traditional, colourful, but above all, relaxed. They take their politics seriously but life less so. Life is for living, to be enjoyed and shared with friends in the form of hospitality; all who visit the island soon become friends.

The Paradise Collection, short stories, are about a village, or rather the growing town of *Kato Laris* and some of its inhabitants. You won't be able to find it on any map of Cyprus because it does not really exist. But it is as real to me, along with its people, as Aphrodite herself. Some of it may be true, a great deal of it could be true, but in the end it is up to you to decide what to believe!

Published by KYRIAKOU